KINGPIN
LEGAL LESSONS FROM
THE UNDERWORLD

SARAH BARTHOLOMEUSZ

The best insights for disrupting the system often come from unexpected places. This book entertains while it informs; a peephole into an underworld of high stakes, where earning respect and loyalty requires confidence, adaptability, but also intimidation, violence, distrust, shifting alliances and excessive management of increasing risk. Competition lurks in every corner, waiting to exploit the smallest opportunity to advance in the power hierarchy. This intense business environment challenges its leaders to innovate to survive while gently poking us to consider the moral, legal and business lessons for success.

Dr Kristin Alford, Futurist, innovator, science communicator and leader of UniSA's Sci■C■Ed studio

Does the absence of a moral code help or hinder criminal organisations, whose leaders rely on violence, extortion, bribery and duplicity to achieve underworld goals? *Kingpin: Legal Lessons from the Underworld* offers insight into the business operations of the drug trade, where innovation and risk management trump corporate governance and compliance.

Dr Catherine Ball, CEO and Founder, Remote Research Ranges Pty Ltd

Visionary business leaders chase higher aspirations, applying their capabilities to a broader range of challenges and loftier goals. Author Sarah Bartholomeusz convinces the reader to cast aside conventional ideas of business role models, enter the underground tunnel of international drug smuggling, and embrace the new curriculum of Kingpin 101.

Caroline Kennedy, CEO, Virtual Executive and author of *The Power of Wow! Why Thank You Makes Dollars & Sense*

American gangster Frank Lucas rose to power in the New York heroin trade by employing an arsenal of effective business practices. In an easy-to-read style, this book explains how Lucas ended the Italian Mafia's monopoly over the Harlem heroin supply by establishing a direct source to high-quality raw opium imported from the Golden Triangle. You will learn about Lucas's innovative smuggling methods, focus on customer service, and innate understanding of the importance of branding the superior grade product he called 'Blue Magic'.

Christine Moody, Brand Expert + Designer Advocate + Experienced Entrepreneur, author *Designer Law School: Legal lessons for design entrepreneurs*

This book proves there is truly something to learn from everyone. A compelling window into the Kingpins who risk everything, even though they have literally everything to lose – there are serious legal lessons here for the corporate world as well as true crime stories that will capture the rest of us. Both an innovative concept, and a well-written book!

Andrea Clarke, CEO at CareerCEO.com.au | Former Washington D.C. News Correspondent

This book engagingly relates the innovative activities of eight Kingpins back to risk management, team building and stakeholder management; these activities are all very relevant regardless of what business you immerse yourself in. By taking these usually dry topics and referencing them to real-life situations, it brings the lessons to life and shows the reader how important the art of storytelling really is.

Gail Creighton-Davies, Director, Rhapsodate Consulting

Steve Jobs (Apple), Sir Richard Branson (Virgin Group), Oprah Winfrey (Harpo Productions), Bill Gates (Microsoft) and Jeff Bezos (Amazon) consistently top the lists of today's most successful, innovative and inspirational business leaders. If we measured success purely by profit, these visionary leaders might in fact be usurped by nefarious Kingpins like Pablo Escobar, Joaquín ('El Chapo') Guzmán and Khun Sa. This riveting book abandons the boardroom for the dark underbelly of the illicit drug trade, where you will meet some of the world's most street smart, wealthiest and reckless Kingpins, and through their stories learn about practices to implement (and not to implement) to gain business advantage.

David Chuter, Chief Executive Officer, Innovation in Manufacturing CC Ltd

Educational and gripping. Not words normally associated with risk and compliance, but Ms Bartholomeusz exceeds on both accounts in this remarkably innovative and thoroughly researched book.

Jamie Tan, Founder & Psychosomatic Practitioner at The Spacious Nest

I urge you to pick up *Kingpin* and expose yourself to a whole new perspective on business risk and compliance – such a fascinating insight into a rarely explored 'industry', especially for business intelligence. You will not regret it.

Paul Smith, Chief Executive Officer, The Future Directors Institute

This book takes a simple idea – that the underworld can inform the corporate world – and provides concrete, accessible and incredibly powerful examples. Sarah writes in an engaging, enthusiastic and well-informed way.

Clarissa Raywald, The Happy Family Lawyer, author of
Splitsville: How to separate, stay out of court and stay friends

A memorable and original take on the stories of infamous drug dealers; it takes courage to lead any business but when risk means losing your life it's a whole new perspective.

Howard Tinker, author and CEO of Restaurant Profits, specialist marketing company for the hospitality industry

Innovation keeps things interesting. Makes for a better world. Just ask Jobs, Tesla, Edison. But who would have thought it made for a better underworld?!

Tim Ried, Host of The Small Business Big Marketing Show and author of *The Boomerang Effect*

Until I read *Kingpin*, I did not appreciate the rate of innovation that occurs in the underworld; combining the eight Kingpins in the book with legal lessons for the corporate world made this both an entertaining and insightful read. Sarah has managed to make reading about the risk, compliance and the law actually entertaining! Highly recommended!

Michael Wilcynski, Director of Accodex Partners

Finally, a book that puts risk and compliance into perspective. *Kingpin* is an excellent (and surprisingly entertaining) resource for anyone undertaking a governance role and looking for context around policy development and application. Sarah's outside-the-square examination of this high-risk, high-reward, significant-consequences environment holds important lessons for legitimate businesses.

Paul Daniel, Director of Ag in Compliance

Organisations today often fail to clearly articulate their risk management framework because they do not take into account that it is a crucial part of their innovation process. Sarah reminds us that legal and compliance lessons can be learned from unexpected innovators that operate in the underworld. *Kingpin* provides a novel approach, offering a practical guide for developing a risk management framework from the most unlikely of teachers!

Lisa Cook, Founder & Managing Director, Get On Board

Sarah's new book highlights an industry and a criminal society where from the outside world rules appear not to exist, yet how do drug lords define any structure or business methodology to create hugely successful global enterprises? The genius of this book is that, whilst not condoning their behaviour, Sarah explores how some of the most notorious criminal CEOs in history have managed to develop incredibly sophisticated commercial operations, and then relates that back to what we can learn from their success and challenges.

Samuel Conway, CEO of Zegami Limited

The legal implications of selecting the illegal drug trade as your industry are obvious, however the parallels to those operations against a corporate setting are so very well described by Sarah in *Kingpin: Legal Lessons from the Underworld*. For those of us used to operating in the latter environment this book offers us a legitimate, albeit voyeuristic entry into this dark world. At times the book is entertaining in its narrative while surreptitiously delivering a lesson in risk management. Thoroughly enjoyed every page.

Karen Ross, General Manager Business Innovation, Elders Ltd

Finally, a book that puts risk and compliance into perspective. You will feel confident and inspired to take your business to new and exciting heights after devouring this informative guide.

Eric Rundall, Chief Financial Officer, Futuris Automotive

For my toddlers Alexander and Nicola:
I'm with you till the end of the line.

THANK
YOU

To the brave souls who freely choose to walk behind, ahead of and beside me; who toil in the dark hours to keep me safe from harm on our journey to a world that is more gentle and just.

You are my rock, my refuge and my shield.

Always know that every good that flows from my hand is the image of your love made manifest.

Project management and text design by Michael Hanrahan Publishing
Cartoons by Daniel Corcoran, Characteristix
Cover design by Peter Reardon

Disclaimer

CONTENTS

FOREWORD

PROFESSOR ROY GREEN BA, LLB, PhD
Dean, UTS Business School, University of Technology Sydney

Innovation is not just an innate factor in human progress but is governed to a large extent by the environment motivating it. In a global economy characterised by ever-lengthening value chains, information overload and accelerated technological change, innovation is a key driver of competitiveness and productivity. How ironic then that criminals are among the first to exploit the vulnerabilities and opportunities that arise from this increasingly complex environment, and to put innovation at the service of their less than admirable deeds. Some years ago, American sociologist, Robert Merton, categorised innovation as a type of deviance and 'a response due to the strain generated by our culture's emphasis on wealth and the lack of opportunities to get rich, which causes people to become "innovators" by engaging in stealing and selling drugs. Innovators accept society's goals, but reject socially acceptable means of achieving them (e.g. monetary success is gained through crime).'

In this very accessible book, Sarah Bartholomeusz takes you to the controversial but radically innovative underworld of the 'Kingpins'. You will be able to analyse the Kingpins' business decisions and extract valuable lessons that more conventional business leaders cannot teach. When we suspend moral judgement, we are presented with a unique opportunity to learn technical skills from innovators playing for high stakes in an extreme environment. The lessons are twofold. To begin with, Kingpins operate in an environment of high political volatility, where loyalties shift rapidly and policy positions are malleable. Moreover, Kingpins face far greater personal risks in their entrepreneurial ventures. When most of us take risks to innovate, we may lose an opportunity, a job or profits, but Kingpins are in danger of losing their freedom or even their lives.

After reading *Kingpin*, you will understand that despite the immoral, destructive and violent culture of the illicit drug trade, Kingpins are, first and foremost, entrepreneurs. The most successful Kingpins are single-minded leaders who innovate, adapt, focus on customer service, create a brand, outsource all but their specialised skills, control strategic aspects of distribution, manage risk, hire diverse employees and cultivate relationships to gain a business advantage. The Kingpins could not survive or succeed without implementing business strategies and policies which would be seen as 'best practice' by governments, corporations … and the drug trade.

Operating in these conditions with such high stakes produces the most ruthlessly selective Darwinian business environment on the planet. By observing the behaviour of Kingpins we see that lessons from the underworld can be far more instructive and obvious than they are in everyday life. Kingpins adapt and change to survive, and in that sense, they are the most innovative of entrepreneurs. By suspending your judgement, at least momentarily, you open your mind to the unique value of the Kingpins' ground-breaking approach – their skills, flaws, triumphs and downfalls being magnified by the volatile context shaping their enterprises. You can deny the Kingpins' moral and social legitimacy, but it is much harder to deny the resilience of their business models and the persuasive lessons to be learned from them.

PREFACE

Who are the most innovative and creative business leaders of all time?

This book presents a novel approach to answering this question.

While names such as Thomas Edison, Steve Jobs, Nikola Tesla and Bill Gates are commonly bandied about, and examining the lives of these visionaries certainly provides a context for analysing success and failure, this book proposes that we consider the possibility that the most innovative and creative business leaders of all time do not operate within the usual confines of the business world.

What if they operate in the underworld?

This book will provide an examination of the lives and careers of eight highly notorious but nonetheless successful drug Kingpins.

These eight people have been chosen because they are all high achievers in their field. In terms of real-world impact, they have all made a difference (though certainly not in terms of positive social contribution). This makes them interesting for business leaders to study. While the Kingpins as leaders operate within a similar rule set to executives, they come from widely differing experience bases and they build their businesses in an environment of extreme volatility. Their responses to compliance situations are not curtailed by the law, best practice or – at times – even logic. This makes them some of the most innovative and creative business leaders in the world, for better and for worse, and they therefore provide us with lessons that are simply unavailable through the study of mainstream leaders.

Considering the lives, successes and failures of these Kingpins provides us with an innovation and creativity scope that is far broader than analysing Thomas Edison, Steve Jobs, Nikolas Tesla and Bill Gates, and provides a lens to enable us to see successes and failures with far more clarity.

Kingpin will identify both business and legal lessons that can be learned from the highs and lows of these people, and also discuss the benefit of implementing relevant business policies to satisfy the objectives of those lessons. The power of the analysis comes from the fact that these underworld executives and entrepreneurs operated parallel to the mainstream economy, but had to respond to similar market forces in far more creative ways. Each of them has experimented wildly, and this means that their victories were amplified, and their mistakes were at times quite literally fatal.

Some business industry experts have recognised that successful drug dealers and legitimate entrepreneurs share many similar traits. In a 2002 article published in the *Journal of Labour Economics* ('Drug Dealing and Legitimate Self-Employment'), economist Rob Fairlie contends the same characteristics compelling individuals to become drug dealers as teenagers also compel them to become entrepreneurs as adults. Common characteristics include low risk aversion, entrepreneurial ability and a preference for autonomy.

William Baumol is an influential American economist who has dedicated his career to expanding the role of the entrepreneur in mainstream economic theory. In an article entitled 'Entrepreneurship: productive, unproductive and destructive', Baumol argues that incentives or payoffs by society for different entrepreneurial activities is the key factor in deciding whether entrepreneurship will be allocated in productive or unproductive directions. The allocation of productive entrepreneurship significantly affects the strength of the economy's productivity growth. Accordingly, policy makers have an interest in developing and implementing business policies that provide incentives or reward structures to individuals or companies involved in entrepreneurial activities.

The Kingpins' drug-trafficking enterprises would be considered 'creative destructive' entrepreneurships in society. The criminal entrepreneur's duty involves locating and exploiting 'opportunities', defined as situations where profit is to be made from criminal activity. Criminal or destructive entrepreneurship provides opportunities for other entrepreneurs. Opportunity discovery concerns the production of value, where the entrepreneur determines or influences the resource choices required to generate value. Opportunities for creating novel economic value exist as a result of the demand for goods and services in illegal markets. Entrepreneurs who join illegal markets assume there are competitive flaws reflecting changes in technology, demand or other factors that individuals or groups in an economy attempt to exploit.

Kingpin will explore the entrepreneurial qualities demonstrated by both the Kingpins and legitimate businesses, contrasting their respective roles as 'creative destructive' and 'productive' entrepreneurships. Valuable lessons can be gleaned from the innovative, destructive business practices of the Kingpins. Their lessons serve as a reminder of the stark contrast between the Kingpins' volatile, violent, unpredictable underworld and the relatively controlled environment cultivated by legitimate business organisations. While the Kingpins operate in a constantly evolving state of lawlessness, companies benefit from developing and implementing diverse business policies such as: corporate governance, regulation and compliance; accounting; management; human resources; shareholder; and company and employee code of conduct policies.

The careers of Kingpins Frank Lucas, Khun Sa, Griselda Blanco, Pablo Escobar, Dawood Ibrahim, Joaquín Guzmán and Christopher Coke are considered in this book. These Kingpins achieved unprecedented success in the nefarious underworld they inhabited. To evaluate 'success' in the drug trade, the factors considered include the accumulation of wealth; the pace at which the Kingpins rose to power; innovation in production, logistic and marketing methodologies; sophistication of the supply chain; global market share; geographical reach of their organisation; political partnerships; community leadership; and longevity.

This book is written understanding that the consequences of illicit drug use in the community are severe and widespread, causing permanent physical and emotional damage to users and negatively impacting their families, co-workers, and others with whom they have contact. The intent is not to glamorise or glorify the drug trade or Kingpins who profited and lost from it, but to emphasise there are valuable lessons to be learned from these Kingpins.

Some consider that success in the drug trade is more difficult to achieve than success in legitimate business. The consequences of risk-taking can be severe in the underworld: incarceration, injury or death. Competition with rival drug organisations can end in death, and this is considered a necessary cost of business. The distribution networks require great sophistication because traffickers must move both the product and the profits in secret, while constantly manoeuvring to avoid arrest or death.

The illicit nature and corresponding secrecy of the illegal drug trade and its key figures fosters legend. Conflicting stories have been a complicating factor in the researching of this book. It is not intended to be an academic work, so potential inaccuracies aside, the lessons derived from the folklores and urban legends shared about the Kingpins can be just as useful as a historically accurate narrative.

RISK MANAGER

1 UNDERSTANDING THE ILLEGAL DRUG TRADE

Parallel to the development of the information revolution, there has been a separate, independent economic boom: the illegal drug trade is a global black market dedicated to the cultivation, manufacture, distribution and sale of substances that are subject to drug prohibition laws. Starting out it is interesting to consider what is known about the economic structure and business operations of illicit drug operations, because the same forces have operated on this market as on other markets, but it is unique because it operates within different constraints.

The constraints – primarily being that the participants operate a business that is against the law – mean that the

Kingpins necessarily bring a very high level of creativity to the way they operate. It is the innovation practices implemented that can provide lessons for the corporate world. This book is not sensationalising the illegal drug industry, but it is acknowledging that the creativity employed by these underworld activities can be of use to us.

MARKET SIZE

The obscurity of the global illicit drug market makes it impossible to accurately estimate its size. This is not because the drug market does not behave like most others in terms of supply and demand, but rather because the most basic inputs that are needed for such an estimation – data on production, prices, and quantities exported, imported and consumed – are themselves often estimates and frequently based on insufficient data.

The value of the global illicit drug market for the year 2003 was estimated at US$13 billion at the production level, US$94 billion at the wholesale level, and US$322 billion based on retail prices.[1] (These are the most reliable recent figures available.)

---

1   United Nations Office on Drugs and Crime, *World Drug Report 2005*, United Nations publication, Sales No. E.05.XI.10.

DRUG PRICES

Prices are high because illegal drugs are scarce, but not in the way that diamonds are scarce. Illegal drugs can easily be cultivated in many different regions of the world. They are scarce because they are legally prohibited. Scarcity alone, however, does not cause high prices; high demand also contributes to the high cost. Where suppliers are relatively scarcer than buyers, suppliers have the 'upper hand' (bargaining power) in negotiations over price.

The path any product takes from manufacture to consumption is called the supply chain. As with all products, the price of illegal drugs increases the closer they get to the end consumer.

SIZE AND STRUCTURE OF DRUG ENTERPRISES

The majority of research on the drug trade has focused on retail dealers selling directly to users, presumably because these individuals are easier to engage in research projects. The evidence suggests that dealers at this level make little, if any, profit from their activities because they often are supplying drugs to sustain their own drug habits, not to earn money.

Drug suppliers are diverse, but two types of individuals are identified as being involved in the trade: 'criminal' drug traffickers, with extensive criminal involvement, and 'businessmen' drug traffickers, who – other than their involvement in drug dealing – are relatively law-abiding.

Drug trade businesses include both large-scale criminal syndicates, such as the Mafia or drug cartels, and fluid organisations that connect small groups of independent entrepreneurs able to trust one another through kinship or friendship ties. Common sense suggests that drug dealing enterprises are likely to be smaller than legitimate businesses because of the need to stay hidden from law enforcement agencies. However, as in legitimate business environments, there are advantages to being bigger. Drug dealing enterprises that remain small (but are larger than their competitors) potentially enjoy higher productivity and earnings, and they are not necessarily at greater risk of arrest.

Drug dealing enterprises vary in their degree of permanence. Successful enterprises do not necessarily endure over time but have more flexible structures. Despite large diversity in business operations, enterprises can also be classified by the sophistication of the 'technologies' used to transport drugs. (This will be fleshed out in more detail later in the book.)

INCREASING PROFITABILITY

All businesses can increase profit by increasing sales (growth), increasing the income generated per sale (increasing price), or reducing their outgoing costs. While legal businesses tend to focus on maximising their profit, it has been argued that drug enterprises focus on minimising their risks – which makes it a perfect economic microcosm to analyse for the purposes of this book.

MONETARY AND NON-MONETARY COSTS

The financial investment required to set up and operate a drug enterprise is minimal. The cost of the drugs from source countries is only a small proportion of its retail price. The main monetary costs for drug dealers involve transport of the drug over policed borders, retailers earning above what they could expect in legitimate employment, and product and asset seizures by law enforcement agencies, competitors, customers or employees.

The non-monetary costs of drug dealing are more substantial. They include the risk to the future of the business operation if apprehended by law enforcement, imprisonment and asset seizure, and the risks that come with interacting with other criminals, such as theft and violence.

RISK MANAGEMENT

There is evidence that high-level drug dealers – Kingpins – take active steps to reduce non-monetary costs. Studies show some Kingpins acknowledge violence is bad for business and take steps to avoid it, and that it is possible to operate as a high-level dealer without using violence. The following table sets out some risk management strategies employed by dealers, to give some context to the risk framework they work in.[2]

Some researchers have suggested that many dealers think the risks of operating in the drug market are low, and others have identified that individual dealers have different risk tolerance levels. For example, some dealers go to significant lengths to ensure they are not in contact with the drugs at any point in a deal by employing staff to take on this role, despite the inefficiencies this generates. Others may enjoy the excitement of personally completing drug deals and so involve themselves more closely in operations.

Examples of risk management strategies used by dealers

Type of risk	Risk identified	Interviewee identified risk management strategies
Market risk	Low demand	• No need for strategy because demand was found to be high and stable
Market risk	Low supply	• Find reliable supplier • Identify more than one supplier
Business risk	Financial loss through confiscation	• Separation of cash and drugs • Set up legitimate business

2   A product of The Beckley Foundation Policy Programme, founded and directed by Amanda Feilding. Used with permission.

Type of risk	Risk identified	Interviewee identified risk management strategies
Credit risk	Other dealers stealing drugs/ money	• Threaten violence • Actual violence
Operational risk	Getting caught with drugs/money	• Only buying drugs when a customer is lined up • Limited stockpiling of drugs • Payments to customs officials • 'Sacrifice' of mules • Many mules on one flight carrying small amounts • Employment of staff, e.g. managers, transporters, storers
Operational risk	Attracting attention of police	• Limiting the number of customers • Spending money on rental goods, e.g. rented houses, cars
Operational risk	Police monitoring of operations, including use of informants	• Only work with and sell to known individuals • Using face-to-face communication or calling from a pay phone • Regularly changing phones
Risk to reputation	Inability to enforce contacts	• Threaten violence • Actual violence

EXPANSION

Like all businesses faced with expansion, Kingpins need to consider their supply side and their demand side. A critical challenge in expanding an illegal drugs business is access to a reliable supplier or network of suppliers. Suppliers are a scarce resource at wholesale and importation levels. Having access to multiple suppliers improves dealers' opportunities to maintain and expand their supply.

Some Kingpins have been able to expand simply by operating in the drug dealing environment, by managing their suppliers. Like managers that work in legitimate businesses, they meet other dealers with similar interests and values and ideas for making more money.

Ethnic ties have proved helpful for some dealers in expanding their networks into other cities or countries. Contacts working in legitimate businesses, in particular transport and logistics, have also facilitated expansion of drug enterprises.

———————

Drug traffickers pursue many of the same principles as any legitimate commodity business, and necessarily they are particularly focused on risk. It follows, then, that analysing the careers of eight of history's most successful Kingpins will provide lessons in the implementation of beneficial business strategies and policies.

FRANK LUCAS
"SUPER FLY"

2 FRANK LUCAS

ORIGIN AND NOTORIETY

Born in North Carolina on 9 September 1930, Frank Lucas is an African-American former drug dealer who controlled the Harlem heroin market during the late 1960s and early 1970s. Lucas moved to New York in 1946, and – until he met his mentor Ellsworth 'Bumpy' Johnson – he earned his living hustling pool and committing petty crimes.

Lucas liked to call himself 'Superfly', a reference to the title of a 1972 blaxploitation movie directed by Gordon Parks. Youngblood Priest, the main character in *Superfly*, is an African-American cocaine dealer who devises a plan to leave the drug world by selling 30 kilos of cocaine and using the profits to sustain his lifestyle while searching for a legitimate job. Along the way Priest has several confrontations with corrupt law enforcement.

Lucas claims he learned the drug trade from Ellsworth 'Bumpy' Johnson, an African-American crime boss operating in Harlem. From 1940 to 1968, Bumpy acted as a middleman between the Italian Mafia, who imported drugs from overseas, and gangsters dealing drugs out of Harlem. Whether Lucas was Bumpy's right-hand man or merely a low-ranking employee has been the subject of much conjecture. When Bumpy died in 1968, Lucas positioned himself to take over Bumpy's heroin distribution operation. To acquire control of it, Lucas would have to bypass the Italian Mafia.

Lucas hustled the streets of Harlem with confidence and an upbeat demeanour, and he entered the perilous global drug market with the same self-assurance. With little knowledge of the country or language, Lucas travelled alone to Bangkok, where he met up with United States Army sergeant Leslie 'Ike' Atkinson – nicknamed 'Sergeant Smack' by the Drug Enforcement Administration (DEA) – who was then based in Thailand. Atkinson owned a bar in Bangkok and was well-connected with US Army soldiers stationed in Southeast Asia, to whom he supplied heroin processed from poppies grown in the Golden

Triangle. Lucas wanted to see the heroin manufacturing process first-hand, and he and Atkinson trekked through the jungles of the Golden Triangle to meet with Atkinson's source. Lucas established his own high-quality wholesale heroin connections in Southeast Asia, masterminded the task of transporting the heroin into the United States and, accordingly, successfully removed the need for the Italian Mafia in his operation.

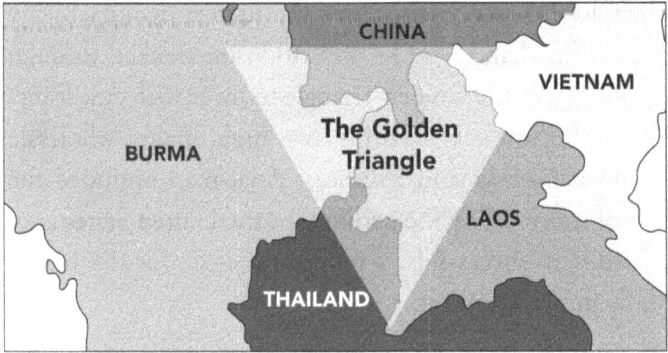

Lucas relied on introspection for innovation. He planned out every detail of his heroin operation, a technique he called 'back tracking'. He would isolate himself in an empty room for weeks at a time to reflect on the various phases of his business. Lucas would mentally perform each step of his operation to look for potential problems. He analysed his past transactions and used his experiences to modify and improve his strategies.

Lucas is known for his innovative smuggling methods. He hid heroin in the pallets underneath American servicemen's coffins, which were loaded onto American military planes and transported from Southeast Asia to the United States. Lucas is also believed to have smuggled heroin in furniture.

Lucas entrusted the sales aspect of his heroin business to a close group of relatives and close friends from North Carolina known as the Country Boys. He believed men recruited from small town origins were less likely to steal from him and would remain loyal.

During the height of his power, Lucas claimed he earned a million dollars a day. There wasn't enough space to hide his cash, so he would personally launder the money, driving large bags of small bills to a bank in the Bronx, where the bankers would sort, count and exchange it for larger bills.

Lucas frequented Harlem's music clubs, where he socialised with famous actors and actresses, musicians, politicians and leaders of the business and crime worlds. Joe Louis, the famous boxer, was one of his best friends.

In 1975, a taskforce comprising New York Police Department detectives and United States DEA agents raided Lucas's home in New Jersey. Although there was no evidence of drugs or guns, paper bags full of uncounted $1 to $20 bills were scattered throughout the house. These small bills, coupled with the fact that Lucas did not work, strengthened the allegation that Lucas was involved in a criminal conspiracy to sell drugs. Lucas was later sentenced to 70 years in prison.

Once convicted, Lucas assisted the authorities and provided evidence which led to 100 additional drug-related convictions. After serving five years in custody, Lucas's sentence was reduced to time served plus lifetime parole. In 1981, he was released from prison and entered a witness protection program. In 1984, Lucas was arrested and convicted of attempting to exchange heroin and money for cocaine. He served a further seven-year prison sentence, and was released in 1991.

Following his final prison release, Lucas returned to Harlem and witnessed the poverty and addiction resulting, in part, from his career pushing drugs. Lucas, who is now wheelchair-bound after a car accident, has spent much of the last decade attempting to repair the damage caused by his drug business. Lucas currently works for his daughter's non-profit organisation Yellow Brick Roads, which provides shelter and resources for children of incarcerated parents.

CAREER HIGHLIGHTS AND LEGAL LESSONS

In the early stages of his career, Lucas demonstrated attributes that would facilitate his rise to power in the heroin industry: attitude and acumen.

Lucas attracted and cultivated diverse relationships

Lucas's primary survival skills were confidence and an upbeat demeanour. He related well to others, attracted a diverse group of friends and business associates, and was considered both a 'man of the people' and a member of an elite network of entertainers, politicians, businessmen and leaders of crime organisations.

Inaction is often the by-product of a fear of the future. Lucas avoided stagnancy by never over-thinking the consequences of his actions. When Lucas identified a business objective, he pursued it with reckless abandon. He believed he could control the lucrative Harlem heroin trade, and his increased expectations drove greater performance.

Despite his inexperience, Lucas confidently navigated the dangers of the international illegal drug trade. He travelled to Southeast Asia to observe the heroin processing and manufacturing process first-hand. In Thailand, he met the drug lord who would become his direct source of raw opium, a man Lucas described as 'an English speaking, Rolls Royce driving Chinese gentleman', living with a paramilitary network of insurgents in the jungles of the Golden Triangle. This atypical but advantageous business relationship is the by-product of innovation bred by diversity.

Lucas's relationships with elite entertainers, athletes and politicians provided a break from the intense demands of his business, and he acquired a respectability not found in the heroin trade. Lucas was well-liked by the members of this powerful social network. They supported his legitimate businesses and invited him to attend charitable events, opportunities that improved his reputation in the community.

Lucas gained peace of mind by entrusting his massive heroin sales operation to the Country Boys. Unlike the majority of his business associates, the Country Boys were a humble, protective, loyal group who focused on customer service and protected Lucas's empire. Lucas's trust in the Country Boys allowed him to focus on other aspects of the business which required his attention.

Lucas's confidence and fearlessness enabled him to attract and cultivate diverse relationships which contributed to his rise to power. Not all leaders or employees have the natural confidence Lucas exhibited, and to ensure that a workplace is dynamic and attractive to people with different skills and experiences, a company can benefit from implementing a **Diversity Policy** that requires the company to encourage and embrace diversity. Evidence has shown that workplaces that are dedicated to ensuring an inclusive environment that encourages and embraces gender, age, ethnic and cultural diversity perform better financially.

Generally, the objectives of a Diversity Policy are to ensure that a company:

- encourages a corporate culture that recognises and values diversity

- provides equal access and opportunities to all its employees
- promotes a fair and balanced approach, ensuring the appointment and advancement of employees is based on skill, performance and capability.

To this end, to ensure these objectives are achieved, discrimination, harassment and victimisation will not be tolerated within the company.

A company that implements a Diversity Policy will recognise the benefits of maintaining diversity among people in a company at all levels in relation to gender, race, ethnicity, disability, age, sexual orientation, gender identity, marital or family status, and religious or cultural background, among others.

Further, a company that implements a Diversity Policy should find that a commitment to diversity in its workforce will contribute to achieving corporate objectives through innovative decision making from people with diverse backgrounds with varying skill sets and perspectives, just as Lucas's team was committed to doing.

Direct sourcing

Lucas demonstrated astute business acumen and the ability to think laterally and clearly, exercise good judgement and make smart decisions for his enterprise. Lucas understood he could not adopt the business model developed by Bumpy, which gave the Italian Mafia a monopoly on supplying heroin. Instead he travelled to Southeast Asia, established his own connections, and procured pure heroin directly from the manufacturer. By purchasing wholesale, Lucas obtained his product at a reduced price and shortened his sales cycle. In cutting out the middleman, Lucas acquired a competitive advantage. Lucas controlled the whole supply chain, from the source to the sale to the end consumer, something none of the other Kingpins achieved.

A company can gain a competitive advantage by implementing a **Wholesale Procurement Policy** which requires the company to source high-quality products and services at a cost that represents the best possible value. The purpose of a policy like this is to provide guidance to company personnel in the purchase of goods and services, and to define the role and responsibilities of each function in the procurement process.

While Lucas may not have focused on the following, a company may also wish to implement this policy to commit to maintaining its high ethical standards, and also take into account its social and environmental responsibilities.

A Wholesale Procurement Policy establishes guidelines for purchasing goods and services and promotes the role of procurement in assisting in acquiring needed goods and services at the best possible value, while also ensuring fairness and openness with all interested suppliers.

A Wholesale Procurement Policy will apply to all company personnel, suppliers and stakeholders, and will focus on:

- purchasing
- risk assessment
- avoiding conflicts
- maintaining confidentiality.

It is widely understood that implementing a Wholesale Procurement Policy and thereby a framework for goods and services procurement reflects best practice principles and arrangements for any business.

Financial failings

Lucas failed to hire appropriate experts to assist with the duties of sorting, counting and laundering the profits from his illegal business. Ironically, as his profit increased, so did his carelessness. Lucas would personally store bags of 'street money' (bills in small denominations received from customers) at his home because he lacked a system to account for and launder cash payments. This negligent practice ultimately contributed to Lucas's demise, as his conviction for drug trafficking relied on evidence that included paper bags full of uncounted cash that were found during a raid of his home.

The preparation of a proper Delegation of Authority can bring efficiency to a business operation. A company can protect its financial health by properly delegating duties to appropriately trained staff. A written **Delegation of Authority Policy** can ensure that leaders of the company are comfortable in delegating tasks to team members. Establishing a clear set of approval limits and strict instructions on the levels of authority that may be delegated, and identifying personnel and employees within a company authorised to engage in activities and make decisions that bind the company, means the leaders can focus on adding as much value as they can.

Additional policies often sit underneath a Delegation of Authority Policy – these can include:

- Travel Expenses Policy
- Corporate Credit Card Policy
- Entertainment & Hospitality Expense Policy & Guidelines
- Purchasing and Procurement Policy
- Sponsorship Policy.

The consequences for Lucas not having a Delegation Policy were severe. Consequences for non-compliance are usually recognised in a Delegation of Authority Policy; for example, not complying can result in the termination of employment.

Planning to win

Lucas used a method that he called 'back tracking' to analyse his strategies and correct the weaknesses within his business operations. He frequently evaluated his illegal drug smuggling strategies and understood the need for constant innovation in this aspect of his operation. While there was significant potential for innovation to boost economic growth, Lucas was also mindful of the risks of innovation.

Organisation, oversight and innovation are important aspects of any business plan. Without innovation, companies risk becoming obsolete. Companies that implement a **Risk Management Policy** adopt a structured and consistent approach to risk management. A Risk Management Policy assists in the alignment of strategy, procedures, people, behaviour and technology for the purpose of evaluating and managing the risks the company faces in creating and protecting shareholder value.

A Risk Management Policy will allow the organisation to adopt a structured and consistent approach to risk management, which will assist in the alignment of strategy, procedures, people, behaviour and technology for the purpose of evaluating and managing the risks the company faces in protecting and creating shareholder value.

Branding

As mentioned earlier, Lucas controlled the whole supply chain, from the source to the sale to the end consumer. He understood two very important business lessons:

1. How to sell and the importance of customer service.
2. The success of business is all about the product.

In the early 1970s the concept of 'branding' was not yet mainstream, but Lucas understood the importance of protecting the reputation of the high-quality heroin he had named 'Blue Magic'.

Customers identified Blue Magic as a very pure, superior product. Lucas was unhappy to learn other drug dealers were purchasing Blue Magic, cutting it with diluting substances, and then reselling it as Blue Magic.

A company can protect its brand (or brands) by implementing a **Customer Service & Complaints Policy** that governs the expectations regarding a product. Such a policy would provide a framework for defining issues such as service delivery standards, the rights of customers, and how complaints from customers will be handled.

Lucas was very customer-focused, and if a company is always focused on its customers and committed to the timely, efficient and consistent delivery of a range of quality services it should flourish. A policy like this will usually include a commitment to ensuring that all customer contact is fair, friendly, informative and efficient. It could also include a commitment to continuous improvement in service delivery to meet the changing needs of a company's customers and the community.

In relation to complaints, this policy could include a commitment to striving to provide a level of service that does not attract complaints, however in the instances where customers are dissatisfied, it would set out a procedure whereby the company would take all possible steps to achieve a resolution.

SUMMARY

Lucas made his mark in the Harlem heroin market. He was a pioneer, and he boldly sought, established and protected a wholesale source for his product, managed risks with organisation and oversight, and implemented innovative smuggling strategies for the continued success of his operation. One flaw in his operation concerned his failure to delegate the financial aspects of the business, an error that ultimately contributed to the end of his reign in Harlem.

3 KHUN SA

KHUN SA'S CRIMINAL CAREER

Notoriety as the 'Opium King'

Khun Sa was born in Mongyai, British Burma on 17 February 1934. In 1989 the country known as Burma changed its name to Myanmar. (This name change has been accepted by the United Nations but not by all nations, however to avoid confusion, the country will be referred to as Myanmar for the rest of this chapter.)

Sa was of mixed Chinese and Shan ethnicity. Shan is a state within Myanmar that borders China to the north,

Laos to the east, and Thailand to the south, and five administrative divisions of Myanmar in the west.

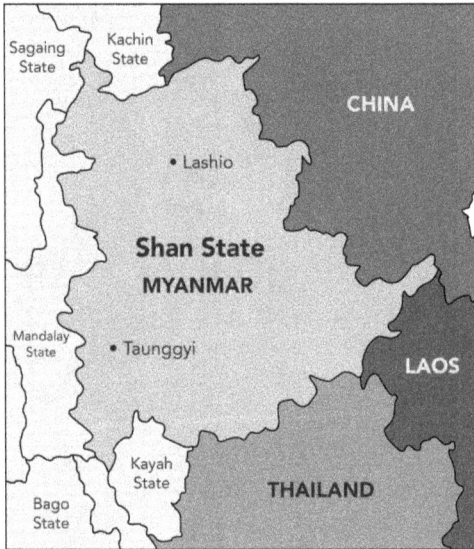

Sa was the Commander-in-Chief of the Mong Tai Army (MTA), a militia comprising armed Shan soldiers who fought to liberate the Shan minority in Myanmar. Sa declared he was a freedom fighter, not a drug dealer, arguing that he supported his army with tax revenues collected from opium traders moving through Shan territory but did not directly profit from drug trafficking himself.

Bert Lintner, an expert in the Southeast Asian drug trade, observed that Sa's Army was, in reality, 'Little more than a narco-army escorting opium convoys and protecting heroin refineries'. United States drug officials contend Sa organised farmers to grow opium and operated or franchised 15 to 20 heroin refining laboratories near the Thai–Myanmar border. Sa reportedly made cash payments to Thai border police to guarantee that his heroin shipments crossed the Thai border without being seized, and then distributed the drug using a sophisticated commercial network.

The Myanmar Government called Sa the 'Opium King' due to his control over such an extensive opium smuggling operation in the Golden Triangle. Sa operated his drug empire for over 30 years and reportedly earned billions of dollars from it. From 1974 to 1994, during Sa's unrivalled dominance of the Shan State, the amount of New York heroin imported from the Golden Triangle rose from 5 percent to 80 percent.

In 1994, it was estimated that Sa and the United Wa State Army collectively controlled 75 percent of the heroin originating from the Golden Triangle. The Wa State Army is the military wing of the United Wa State Party, an ethnic minority army of an estimated 20,000 to 25,000 Wa soldiers. The Wa people are an ethnic group living primarily in northern Myanmar, in the northern part of

Shan State and the eastern part of Kachin State, near and along Myanmar's border with China, as well as in China's Yunnan Province.

Early military experience

Sa's initial military experience was in skirmishes with the Kuomintang (KMT) (nationalist Chinese forces), who had set up bases in Loi Maw, Shan State in the early 1950s. As a leader he started young; when he was only 16 he formed his own army of a few hundred men. In the early 1960s, Sa's private army received money, uniforms and weapons from the Myanmar Government in return for fighting against the Shan rebels. As long as Sa's people fought the KMT, the BCP and other regime foes (for example, legitimate independence movements such as the Shan State Army – SSA), the central government would overlook other activities, principally opium trading.

Shifted alliance to Shan State

Once Sa had gathered an army of 800 soldiers, he declared himself a Shan nationalist and set up his own drug-producing principality.

In 1967, the KMT interfered with Sa's opium trade by blocking his jungle smuggling routes. This started what would become known as the Opium War of 1967, which ended in Sa's demoralising defeat.

In 1969, the Myanmar Government captured Sa when he went to negotiate with Shan rebels, perhaps as a prelude to shifting his alliance from Myanmar to the Shan people. The court convicted Sa of treason for daring to meet with the SSA. Sa was released from prison in 1973 when his followers kidnapped two Russian doctors and demanded their leader's freedom in exchange.

Thailand-based opium operation

By 1976, Sa had returned to opium smuggling, renaming his group the Shan United Army (SUA). They began fighting for Shan autonomy from the Myanmar Government.

After the Myanmar Government broke the KMT's control over the Golden Triangle opium market, the SUA stepped in to take over. Sa established a new headquarters in Thailand. He effectively cut out the 'middle man', procuring his opium directly from Hill tribe and Shan farmers and transporting it to heroin labs in Myanmar, Laos and Yunnan in China, where the final product was turned over to ethnic Chinese syndicates which controlled access to world markets through Thailand, Yunnan and Hong Kong.

In 1981, at the direction of the United States DEA, Thai Rangers and Myanmar guerrillas attempted to assassinate Sa, but he survived the attack. With all the publicity, Thailand could no longer protect Sa. In 1982, after a long and arduous campaign, the Thai military pushed Sa's army back into Myanmar. Sa simply set up a new headquarters just inside Myanmar at Ho Mong (a city in Myanmar and part of the Shan State), from where he controlled the world's heroin trade for nearly two decades.

Formation of Mong Tai Army

In 1985, Sa combined his forces with the 'Tai Revolutionary Council' of Moh Heng, a faction of the Shan United Revolutionary Army, forming the Mong Tai Army. Through that alliance, Sa acquired control of the entire Thai–Myanmar border area from his base at Ho Mong and became a principal figure of opium smuggling in the Golden Triangle.

In 1988, Sa was interviewed by Australian journalist Stephen Rice, who had crossed the border from Thailand into Myanmar illegally. Sa told Rice he was willing to sell his entire heroin crop to the Australian Government for about A$50 million a year for the next eight years, a move that would have virtually stopped the heroin trade into both Australia and the United States overnight. The Australian Government rejected the offer, with Australia Senator Gareth Evans declaring: 'The Australian Government is simply not in the business of paying criminals to refrain from criminal activity.'

Operation Tiger Trap

Sa's problems began in 1994 when Thailand, under pressure from the United States, shut down the drug lord's smuggling routes around his main camps near Homong and Doilang. Thai soldiers were posted along roads, logging trails and even footpaths. In a United States–led operation called Operation Tiger Trap, eleven of Sa's closest aides were arrested by Thai police. Sa's lieutenants were thrown in jail and awaited possible extradition to the United States on drug charges. As a result, Sa had neither supplies nor customer lists, and soon he was running short of money. Over two years, they cut off Sa's access to drugs, money and arms.

In April 1995, the Myanmar army attacked Sa's army. After the attack, two-thirds of Sa's soldiers mutinied, claiming Sa was more interested in the opium trade than independence for the Shan.

Surrender

In 1995, Sa advised Myanmar generals he would retire as commander of the Moi Tang army. In 1996, Sa formally surrendered to the Myanmar generals. He welcomed the leader of the Myanmar army with scotch, and his representatives and those of the Myanmar Government exchanged gifts, posed for photographs and addressed each other with polite honorifics. A ceremony was later held in which 12,000 of Sa's soldiers formally surrendered a cache of 7,500 weapons. Many ethnic Shan nationalists, who had joined Sa's organisation believing that he was a devout Shan patriot, were devastated by his decision to lay down arms.

After the 'surrender', the Myanmar ambassador to Thailand reported Sa would not be extradited to the United States and would be 'dealt with' under Myanmar law. It is believed Sa surrendered to the Myanmar Government to keep the Wa army from overrunning his Doilang Mountain operation on the Thai border and taking over his smuggling routes into Thailand.

Sa was never arrested or investigated by the Myanmar Government. He lived the rest of his life in the Rangoon area, with significant investments in Yangon, Mandalay and Taunggyi, until his death of natural causes in 2007.

Despite his surrender, drugs continued to flow across Myanmar's borders in all directions, demonstrating that the networks Sa created and developed are still very much intact.

CAREER HIGHLIGHTS AND LEGAL LESSONS

Developed a sophisticated army

When Sa assembled his first small army, he lacked funds to clothe, feed and arm his soldiers. Sa, however, was resourceful; he negotiated an agreement with the Myanmar Government whereby Sa's army fought the Shan rebels in exchange for money, uniforms and weapons. Sa wisely took advantage of government backing to consolidate his power and increase the strength of his militia. Once Sa had assembled an army of 800 soldiers, he shifted alliances and claimed his loyalty belonged to the Shan people. Sa funded his new army with profits from the opium trade.

From a young age, Sa knew how to manage and lead large groups of people and keep them in line with a formal or informal **Employee Code of Conduct Policy**, which could encompass a range of other policies. A policy such as this would usually confirm a company's commitment not only to complying with its legal obligations but also to acting ethically and responsibly – although Sa's policy probably did not include this requirement! The policy would usually undertake that the company expects a high level of honesty, care, fair dealing and integrity in the conduct of all business activities, and be an umbrella policy that includes policies such as the following underneath it:

- Confidentiality
- Drug and Alcohol
- Internet and Email
- Safety

- Staff Leave
- Vehicle
- Relationships
- Return to Work
- Online and Social Media
- Anti-Discrimination and Harassment.

Like Sa – who maximised his resources by using government financing to equip, strengthen and expand his army – a company can acquire a competitive advantage by forming alliances with likeminded companies. A company can benefit by implementing a **Productive Partnerships Policy**. Partnerships add value to the work each organisation has already undertaken independently as they share a common vision that leads them to align their separate activities and resources to support their overall goals.

Effective organisations are able to share their vision and goals with others, and this allows them to engage partners in helping to achieve the vision. A Productive Partnerships Policy would encompass strategic partnerships and alliances formed with key partners. It would acknowledge that other collaborative relationships – such as networks, collaborative agreements, funding arrangements and working groups – are important for the operation of the business. In addition to providing a framework for understanding partnerships and collaborative arrangements, a Productive Partnerships Policy would usually include:

- key principles for forming a partnership
- a partnership and collaboration decision matrix
- guidelines for developing, maintaining and dissolving partnerships.

These tools can then be used to help determine if future strategic alliances or formal partnership agreements are appropriate approaches for a particular outcome. While this policy would mainly address strategic partnerships, the key principles, partnership and collaboration selector and partnership guidelines can be considered for most business relationships to ensure that they are functional and effective.

Lack of vision

While Sa was a master of shifting alliances, he could thrive only so long as he balanced the potentially conflicting interests of the competing ethnic rivalries and opium-funded private armies. Sa's surrender to Myanmar troops in 1996 was precipitated by his ill-conceived and grandiose attempt to confront these powers by creating and pledging loyalty to an independent Shan State, an endeavour that brought Sa into simultaneous conflict with Myanmar, Thailand, China and the United States.

Once Thailand and the United States united to eliminate Sa's opium supply line, Sa ran out of funds to support his army, and the defeat of the Shan people was imminent. Sa was forced to surrender and retire from the lucrative drug trade.

Never imprisoned

Sa maintained influence throughout his long career and was never apprehended, arrested or imprisoned. Sa was politically very savvy, and accordingly understood the importance of his own privacy and maintaining the privacy of his associates.

A **Privacy Policy** is required by businesses with a turnover of more than A$3 million, and some companies that operate within specific industries. If required, a Privacy Policy should be implemented to confirm a company's commitment to the importance of keeping personal information private.

The policy must be aligned with the Australian Privacy Principles as set out in the *Privacy Act 1988* (Cth), which describes the way that personal information may be collected, held and disclosed.

SUMMARY

Khun Sa's rise to power in the Golden Triangle opium trade can be attributed to his ability to build a sophisticated army which overpowered and outlasted his competitors. He manipulated and maximised his resources to sustain his army, shifting alliances whenever necessary to acquire an advantage within the opium trade. Sa's decline in power can be attributed to a lack of vision and poor leadership. His professed allegiance to the Shan State brought him into simultaneous conflict with Myanmar, Thailand, China and the United States, who joined forces to cut off his opium supply line. As Sa's opium network disintegrated, the Shan people began to doubt his commitment to their cause. Despite the loss of his lucrative opium empire, Sa succeeded in avoiding arrest and extradition after he surrendered to the Myanmar Government.

4 GRISELDA BLANCO

GRISELDA BLANCO'S ORIGIN AND RISE TO POWER

Born in Cartagena, Columbia on 15 February 1943, Griselda Blanco trafficked drugs for Columbia's Medellín Cartel. The Medellín Cartel was an organised network of drug suppliers and smugglers originating in the city of Medellín, Columbia. She is thought to have been Columbia's first female drug lord.

During the 1970s and early 1980s, Blanco pioneered both the New York and Miami-based cocaine trades and operated one of the largest cocaine distribution networks in the United States. Blanco was notoriously ruthless and allegedly responsible for up to 200 murders committed while transporting cocaine from Colombia to New York, Miami and Southern California.

Childhood

Raised in poverty by an abusive mother, Blanco resorted to petty crime and prostitution to survive. At age 11 she kidnapped a 10-year-old boy, and when his family refused to pay the ransom she demanded, she brutality murdered him. This anecdote has caused speculation that Blanco's propensity for violence was innate.

When Blanco was a teenager she met her first husband, Carlos Trujillo, a street hustler and counterfeiter who sold fraudulent immigration papers. Blanco learned the basics of running a criminal enterprise from Trujillo. They had three children together before divorcing in the late 1960s. A few years later, Blanco reportedly had him killed over a drug dispute.

For over two decades, Blanco worked for the Medellín Cartel as a key distributor. Known as the 'Godmother of Cocaine', Blanco was the first Columbian drug lord to export cocaine to the United States.

New York operation

In the early 1970s, Blanco and her second husband, Alberto Bravo, moved to New York City and developed a successful cocaine enterprise. Prior to their arrival, the Italian Mafia largely controlled New York's drug distribution. With a direct connection to Columbian cocaine, Blanco and Bravo soon captured a large share of the market.

In New York, Blanco developed a sophisticated cocaine operation. Blanco and Bravo masqueraded as successful business people. Blanco recruited and trained young women to act as mules (a practice she is said to have pioneered), operate New York stash houses and transport money to Columbia. Money was laundered via small deposits made in New York, New Jersey and Columbian banks. Blanco also designed and created specialised women's undergarments and luggage to facilitate smuggling cocaine.

However, the operation soon attracted the attention of law enforcement, who gathered evidence against Blanco and Bravo in a sting called 'Operation Banshee'. In 1975, they were indicted on federal drug conspiracy charges. At the time, it was the largest cocaine case in history. Blanco left New York and fled to Columbia before she could be arrested, using her document forgery skills to assume a new identity.

Once in Columbia, she arranged to meet Bravo to discuss a dispute over money missing from their New York operation. When they started to argue, a gun fight ensued that ended when Blanco shot Bravo dead, thereby eliminating one of the most feared drug lords in the Columbian cocaine business. It was a major step in Blanco's rise to power as a cold-blooded crime lord, as she was now the undisputed leader of her operation.

Evading arrest

Blanco evaded capture for approximately ten years after she was indicted on drug charges arising from her dealings in New York. DEA agents tracked Blanco to Colombia and believed she would not travel to the United States. At the time, Columbian laws prohibited extradition of its citizens to the United States to face criminal charges. As long as Blanco remained in Columbia, United States agents could not arrest her and compel her to stand trial in an American court.

Blanco was skilled at hiding in the mainstream. She was neither well known nor readily identifiable as a drug trafficker by either the public or authorities.

Miami operation

In the late 1970s, Blanco, still a fugitive, returned to the United States to rebuild her cocaine empire in Miami. The Miami cocaine market was thriving when Blanco arrived. She wasn't satisfied, however, with merely joining the drug game. She wanted to control it.

Blanco acquired a monopoly on the market using sheer violence, orchestrating a killing spree designed to eradicate her rival dealers and eliminate all competition. Blanco's extreme ruthlessness paid off, as she cornered the market, operating a coast-to-coast distribution network and earning US$80 million a month in illegal drug profits.

Like other female drug traffickers, Blanco established key alliances with men to develop a successful cocaine enterprise. However, Blanco differed from other female Kingpins in her attitude, with frequent use and brutal displays of violence. Blanco used violence to assert her authority and intimidate men working in the drug trade (both competitors and members of her own cartel). A friend of Blanco's suggested that Blanco 'wore murder as a badge of honour; both killing to preserve status and honour in the organisation'.

Blanco used cocaine, and was reported by many to be extremely mentally unstable. She threw wild parties with prostitutes and an endless supply of drugs. She was openly bisexual and engaged in numerous affairs with both men and women, which led to a lot of drama. Eventually, the violence and fast lifestyle choices took their toll. With cocaine fuelling her paranoia, she retreated for long periods behind the gates of her mansion.

Arrest and imprisonment

Blanco acquired a lot of enemies as a result of her brutal tactics, and by 1984 she was forced to leave Miami after numerous assassination attempts by her rivals. She moved to California to hide from them, and to break into the West Coast drug markets. In 1985, the DEA arrested Blanco at her Irvine residence for crimes relating back to drug activity in New York. She was convicted and sentenced to over a decade in prison, but continued to operate her drug empire with the help of her boyfriend and protégé, Charles Cosby.

Retirement from the drug trade

After being released from prison in 2004, Blanco was deported to Columbia. She gave up her life of crime and lived comfortably on the wealth and property she had maintained from her empire. She lived a relatively quiet life until 2012, when at 69 years old she was killed outside a butcher shop in Medellín by gunmen riding motorcycles. Local radio reported that she received two shots to the head. Ironically, she was the victim of what has been speculated to be a revenge killing, performed in a manner she invented herself.

CAREER HIGHLIGHTS AND LEGAL LESSONS

Rise to power

Blanco's rise to power as the largest cocaine distributor in America was due in large part to her strategic acts of ruthless violence and her sophisticated business operation. Blanco's drug empire continued to flourish despite her imprisonment, indicating the strength of her operation.

Blanco consistently operated by her own Code of Conduct, one committed to violence and intimidation. Companies can benefit from adopting a structured **Company Code of Conduct Policy** setting out the company's commitment to complying with its legal obligations, acting ethically and responsibly, and conducting all its business activities with a high level of honesty, care, fair dealing and integrity.

A Company Code of Conduct is defined as the 'principles, values, standards, or rules of behaviour that guide the decisions, procedures and systems of an organisation in a way that (a) contributes to the welfare of its key stakeholders, and (b) respects the rights of all constituents affected by its operations'. Business leaders can identify the character or ethical standards of the company in this code.

The concept of a Company Code of Conduct refers to policy statements that define ethical standards for the organisation's conduct. There is a great variance in the ways these statements are drafted. They can take a number of formats and address many issues, including setting the minimum standards of conduct expected of all directors, officers, executives, employees and contractors of the company. Company Codes of Conduct are completely voluntary.

Blanco continued to successfully operate her drug empire while she was imprisoned in the United States. A company faced with the absence or incapacitation of a board member could benefit by implementing a **Board Charter**. A Board Charter will clearly define the respective roles, responsibilities and authorities of the board of directors (both individually and collectively) and management in setting the direction, management and control of the organisation. Additional purposes of a Board Charter include promoting high standards of corporate governance and enabling the Board to provide strategic guidance and effective oversight of the management of the company.

The creation and protection of shareholder value is an additional important aspect of a Board Charter; it will usually describe what the board and directors are responsible for and outline the Committees of the Board as well.

Blanco's attitude of violence in the underworld is akin to anti-competitive behaviour in the legitimate world of business. The *Competition and Consumer Act 2010* covers most areas of the market, including the relationships between suppliers, wholesalers, retailers and consumers. Its purpose is to enhance the welfare of Australians by promoting fair trading and competition, and through the provision of consumer protections. Many companies will confirm their commitment to complying with this legislation through a Company Code of Conduct. While not intended to be exhaustive, such a code will set the minimum standards of conduct expected of all directors, officers, executives, employees and contractors of a company.

Instability

Blanco's propensity for violence escalated when she arrived in Miami. Increased competition, fear of further surveillance, and her fugitive status contributed to Blanco's stress. She was a heavy cocaine user, which often caused her to lose control.

Blanco's enterprise suffered as a result of her drug use and mental instability. Substance abuse commonly seeps into the everyday operations of businesses and can have a dramatic effect on employee productivity. A company can benefit by implementing a **Drug and Alcohol Policy**, which can protect your company from safety liabilities.

A Drug and Alcohol Policy will vary from business to business, depending on the business's operations; for example, it is appropriate for some businesses to have a zero tolerance policy towards illegal drug use and alcohol abuse. It is commonly accepted that alcohol and other substances may impair the ability of a staff member to perform their duties effectively and safely.

A Drug and Alcohol Policy may also include a right for the company to request a drug or alcohol test of any employee based upon a reasonable suspicion that the employee is under the influence of alcohol or illicit drugs. A reasonable suspicion may include, but is not limited to, physical evidence of use, a substantial drop in work performance, unusual or erratic behaviour, or involvement in a workplace accident.

If an employee returns a positive test result there may be a sanction imposed; for example, the employee may be required to leave their workplace immediately. Usually a positive test result will lead to disciplinary action, which could potentially include immediate termination of employment.

Blanco had a propensity for violence. This behaviour was consistent towards her staff and loved ones – it was part of her usual modus operandi. A policy committing to **Anti-Discrimination and Bullying** can ensure that your staff know you are committed to maintaining a safe and supportive workplace. Such a policy would usually confirm the company's commitment to open discussion and accountability in all relationships.

Unlike the staff who worked for Blanco, most companies will make a commitment to all employees that they have the right to feel safe in their place of work. Further, the policy will undertake that no person may be mistreated, discriminated against, harassed or abused on any grounds whatsoever, including race, religion or gender. It is recommended that all companies implement a policy confirming their commitment to providing a workplace free from all forms of harassment, discrimination and bullying.

Ability to evade law enforcement

Whether they were motivated by fear or respect, Blanco had the loyalty of her employees. She operated her enterprise for decades without any of her employees blowing the whistle on her operation. Employee loyalty facilitated Blanco's ability to stay below the radar of law enforcement and the continued growth of her drug trafficking operation.

All companies can benefit from implementing a **Confidentiality Policy** to protect business, management and employee information. Failing to properly secure and protect confidential business information can lead to the loss of business/clients. The disclosure of sensitive employee and management information can lead to a loss of employee trust, confidence and loyalty, which almost always results in a loss of productivity.

A Confidentiality Policy will recognise that employees are privy to large amounts of personal and commercial information relating to the activities of the business that they work for. In such a policy, a company will confirm that in order to preserve shareholder value it is committed to preserving and protecting all confidential and sensitive information of the company, employees, customers, agencies, related entities and business relationships.

Blanco was fortunate to not have any of her team report her activities to the authorities. Companies that operate within the usual constraints of the law can provide employees with protection for blowing the whistle on fraudulent or corrupt activities. An **Anti-Corruption and Whistleblower Policy** can protect the leaders of a company because it is a declaration that the board has a zero tolerance level for fraudulent or corrupt activities.

An Anti-Corruption and Whistleblower Policy reinforces a company's commitment to the identification, management and prevention of fraudulent or inappropriate activities. Such a policy will provide a framework for the conduct of investigations to ensure that all suspected fraudulent and corrupt activity is appropriately investigated, and confirm that the company is committed to the protection of whistleblowers from adverse consequences.

SUMMARY

Blanco will be remembered as a ruthless Columbian cocaine distributor who consistently adhered to her own Code of Conduct promoting violence and intimidation. Despite her fugitive status following an indictment on drug charges in New York, Blanco relocated to Miami, where she continued to expand her distribution network and increase her share of the US cocaine market. Blanco eliminated competition by killing off her rivals, flew under the radar of law enforcement by sustaining employee loyalty, and continued to operate her vast cocaine enterprise even after she was incarcerated.

Blanco's loss of power coincided with her accumulation of enemies, many of whom sought to avenge murders committed by Blanco. Excessive cocaine use fuelled her paranoia, instability and loss of control. She was the target of so many assassination attempts she eventually could not leave her Miami mansion without fear of being executed. Blanco was forced to relocate to California, a decision which ultimately contributed to the end of her dominance in the cocaine underworld.

PABLO ESCOBAR
"THE WORLD'S GREATEST
OUTLAW"

5 PABLO ESCOBAR

ORIGIN AND RISE TO POWER

Born in Rionegro, Columbia on 1 December 1949, Pablo Emilio Escobar Gaviria, most commonly known as Pablo Escobar, was a Columbian drug lord and one of the world's most notorious Kingpins. He was a founder and, eventually, the head of the Medellín Cartel in Columbia. In the early 1990s, Escobar was the wealthiest criminal in history and one of the 10 richest men in the world, with an estimated known net worth of US$30 billion. At the peak of his career, Escobar earned an estimated US$420 million per week in revenue, supplying 15 tons of cocaine per day to the United States and controlling an estimated 80 percent of the global cocaine market. This earned him the nickname the 'World's Greatest Outlaw'.

Early life

From an early age, Escobar demonstrated an unusual drive and ambition to rise above his modest beginnings. As a young man, he told his friends and family he wanted to become President of Colombia. Pablo was accepted at the Universidad Autónoma Latinoamericana of Medellín, but he couldn't pay his tuition and dropped out in 1966.

In the early 1970s, Escobar worked as a petty street thief, stealing cars and selling contraband cigarettes. Escobar's early success came during the 'Marlboro Wars', in which he played a principal role in the control of Colombia's smuggled cigarettes. Escobar began to believe a life of crime could bring him wealth and legitimacy.

In the mid 1970s Escobar partnered with Jorge Ochoa, who came from a wealthy family dealing in the cattle-breeding and family restaurant businesses. Escobar and Ochoa briefly operated a marijuana-growing business before expanding into the cocaine business. Griselda Blanco reportedly mentored Escobar when he was new to the cocaine trade, but there is little evidence of their relationship.

In 1975, Escobar began developing his cocaine operation. He started smuggling coca paste from Peru into Colombia, where it was processed. Also in 1975, Escobar reportedly ordered the murder of Fabio Ochoa Restrepo, a successful Medellín cocaine trafficker, and then advised Restrepo's men that they would now work for him.

In 1976, Escobar and some of his men were arrested in Medellín after police officers caught them with 39 pounds of coca paste smuggled into Colombia from Ecuador. Escobar unsuccessfully attempted to bribe Medellín judges to dismiss his case. After several months of legal proceedings, Escobar had the two arresting officers killed; the crime was investigated but eventually the authorities abandoned the case. This was the start of a new reign by Escobar; from this point he took control by either killing or bribing those in power.

CAREER OVERVIEW

Formation of the Medellín Cartel

By 1978, Escobar and Ochoa monopolised the majority of cocaine production in Medellín. In the late 1970s, they formed the Medellín Cartel. The founders were Pablo Escobar, José Gonzalo Rodríguez and the Ochoa brothers: Jorge, Juan David and Fabio. The Medellín Cartel procured their coca from Bolivia and Peru and processed it in Colombia. They contracted with American pilots to fly the cocaine from Colombia into the United States.

It was in the 1980s that the Medellín Cartel's infamy grew both at home and abroad. At this time the Medellín Cartel was understood to be controlling around 80 percent of Bolivian and Peruvian consignments that entered the United States, Mexico, Puerto Rico and the Dominican Republic. Escobar's merchandise was also accessed by people in many other countries, mostly around the Americas, however some have said that Escobar's contacts reached as far as Asia.

Soon the Medellín Cartel was more powerful than the national government. The cartel employed corruption and intimidation to stifle their rivals and the authorities. Escobar called his ruthless policy towards judges, police and political officials 'plata o plomo' ('silver or lead'). He first offered generous bribes (silver), and if the bribe was refused, Escobar simply had the person shot (lead). During the 1980s, the cartel killed thousands of police, judges and politicians, including three presidential candidates.

At the height of his power, Escobar enjoyed considerable public popularity and influence. He elicited public support by portraying himself as a gentle and humble friend of the poor. He was a natural at public relations and cultivated a 'Robin Hood' persona by sponsoring charities and football clubs, and paying for low-income housing, hospitals, schools and other necessities for the impoverished Medellín community.

In the late 1980s, the Medellín Cartel controlled most of the world's illegal drug markets. The organisation had fleets of planes, boats, expensive vehicles and a private army.

It was bringing in an estimated US$30 billion annually at its zenith.

Political life

In 1982, Escobar obtained a seat in the Congress of Columbia and convinced the Columbian Constitutional Party to ban the extradition of Columbian criminals to the United States. Escobar feared being extradited to the United States because he had no political influence there and knew American officials would refuse his bribes and requests for preferential treatment.

As an elected official Escobar was thrust into the spotlight, and the media started investigating the source of his wealth. The press discovered Escobar's ties to the drug industry, and the Columbian Government was compelled to take action. Eventually Escobar's congressional seat was revoked. US officials revoked Escobar's visa. In retaliation, Escobar orchestrated a reign of domestic terrorism against the government officials, journalists and civilians who exposed his ties to crime. The violence was so brutal it eventually turned the public against him.

Threat of extradition

In 1990, the United States Government exerted pressure on the Columbian Government to extradite members of the Medellín Cartel for prosecution on drug charges. Faced with the prospect of extradition, Escobar started kidnapping prominent Colombians and killing those who supported extradition of Columbian criminals to the United States.

The Colombian Government and Escobar's lawyers negotiated a deal whereby Escobar agreed to surrender to Columbian authorities and serve a five-year jail term. In return, he would build his own prison and avoid extradition to the United States or anywhere else.

La Catedral

Escobar built his own prison, La Catedral, a stylish structure featuring a Jacuzzi, waterfall, full bar and soccer field. Escobar was the only inmate in La Catedral. He selected his own 'guards' and continued to operate his organisation inside La Catedral by delivering orders over the phone.

In 1992 Escobar ordered his men to bring four members of the rival Cali Cartel to La Catedral to be tortured and executed. The President of Colombia learned of the executions and instructed the Columbian army to remove Escobar from La Catedral and relocate him to a Columbian prison. Again fearing extradition to the United States, Escobar escaped from La Catedral before the army arrived and went into hiding.

Hunt for Escobar

The United States Government helped coordinate an extensive manhunt. By late 1992, two organisations were searching for Escobar: the Search Bloc (a US-trained Colombian special task force) and Los PEPEs ('People Persecuted by Pablo Escobar' – an organisation financed by Escobar's primary rival, the Cali Cartel, comprising family members of Escobar's victims).

In pursuit of Escobar, Los PEPEs hunted down and killed Escobar's friends, contacts and associates. Escobar evaded his captors for approximately 16 months, until authorities traced a telephone call he made from a Medellín safe house. On 2 December, 1992, Escobar was shot and killed in a gun battle on the rooftop of his safe house. The death of Pablo Escobar marked the end of the powerful and ruthless Medellín Cartel.

CAREER HIGHLIGHTS AND LEGAL LESSONS

The success of the Medellín Cartel depended on the collective skills of its members and leader, Pablo Escobar. Escobar's rise to power in the cocaine trade can be attributed to his ability to control the distribution chain, adapt his business model to maximise profits, and influence the Medellín community and his opponents.

Controlling the distribution chain

Escobar specialised in planning, building and organising distribution routes for his product. He controlled the entire distribution chain, from procurement of raw materials to delivery of the product to the end consumer. Escobar owned fleets of airplanes, ships and trucks to transport his product. Escobar's distribution chain was so efficient, even Escobar's competitors hired him to take their products out of Columbia. Escobar understood he couldn't trust distribution to third parties and, accordingly, controlled all facets of his distribution chain.

Escobar understood a company should never outsource its core competencies. A company could implement this lesson by adopting a **Procurement Policy**. A Procurement Policy will provide guidance to company personnel in the purchase of goods and services and to define the role and responsibilities of each function in the procurement process, with the objective of ensuring the company sources high-quality products and services at a cost that represents the best possible value, while maintaining the organisation's high ethical standards and taking into account social and environmental responsibilities. A Procurement Policy will provide guidance to company personnel in the purchase of goods and services and define the role and responsibilities of each function in the procurement process. A Procurement Policy not only ensures the company sources high-quality products and services at a cost that represents the best possible value, but it also maintains the organisation's high ethical standards, taking into account social and environmental responsibilities.

A Procurement Policy can establish guidelines for purchasing goods and services and promote the role of procurement in assisting in acquiring needed goods and services at the best possible value.

Adaptability

Escobar demonstrated an ability to adapt his business model to maximise profits. Before trafficking in cocaine, Escobar worked as a petty street thief, smuggling contraband such as tobacco and liquor. Escobar soon realised he increased his risk by transporting large quantities of a product, and that he could make more money selling a suitcase full of cocaine than a truck full of tobacco and whiskey. Escobar's cocaine business further evolved when he expanded distribution into America, where a less competitive and more profitable cocaine market existed. Escobar was able to pivot and adapt his business model (smuggling cocaine instead of tobacco and liquor; expanding distribution of cocaine to the US market) to maximise his profits.

In Australia, organisations with a significant focus on logistics – like Escobar's – need to consider the Chain of Responsibility legislation that plays an important role in ensuring all parties in the road transport supply chain are aware of their obligations under road transport legislation, and understand how their actions can affect road transport worker safety. If there is an incident under the Heavy Vehicle National Law, the only defence to a breach is if a company has taken 'all reasonable steps' to prevent a breach from occurring.

At the most comprehensive end of the spectrum, a company may have a detailed **Chain of Responsibility Policy and Procedure**, which would usually include:

- statement of intent
- operations
- specific details of what steps are required to be taken in all reasonably anticipated circumstances in order to achieve compliance
- specific detail as to how compliance with the mandated steps will be monitored and measured
- specific sanctions or remedial action that will be imposed or taken in the event of non-compliance.

Following these steps in preparing Policies and Procedures will not leave anything to chance, and they will provide express and detailed guidance to individuals as to what is required in any likely situation.

Depending on your company operations, a **Dangerous Goods Storage and Handling Policy** could be appropriate, particularly if your company – like Escobar's – deals with dangerous goods. Dangerous goods are classified as substances, mixtures or articles that, because of their physical, chemical (physicochemical) or acute toxicity properties, present an immediate hazard to people, property or the environment. Types of substances classified as dangerous goods include explosives, flammable liquids and gases, corrosives, and chemically reactive or acutely (highly) toxic substances. This area is highly regulated, and the criteria used to determine whether substances are classified as dangerous goods are contained in the Australian Code for the Transport of Dangerous Goods by Road and Rail (ADG Code). The ADG Code contains a list of substances classified as dangerous goods. State and Territory workplace dangerous goods storage and handling laws also capture combustible liquids. Many dangerous goods are also classed as hazardous substances.

A policy covering Dangerous Goods Storage and Handling would provide company staff with guidelines on the storage and handling of dangerous goods, including the requirement for notification to authorities when exceeding the threshold.

Influence

Escobar practised philanthropy to influence the Medellín community and violence to influence his opponents.

If a company participates in charitable events, it can benefit by implementing a **Sponsorship Policy** which sets forth a consistent policy on evaluation criteria in relation to potential sponsorship deals by the company. The purpose of a Sponsorship Policy is to maintain consistency, transparency and efficiency in assessing and approving sponsorships.

A **Corporate Social Responsibility Policy** is recommended to assess and take responsibility for the company's effects on environmental and social wellbeing. This policy enables a company to confirm its commitment to attaining the highest standards in ethical, responsible and sustainable business practices. While this may not have been what Escobar was aiming for, many companies recognise that Corporate Social Responsibility touches every part of the business and encourages all stakeholders to contribute to the vision of significantly reducing the impact on the environment and supporting the communities.

A CSR program will usually focus on four key areas where the company is seeking to make a difference:

- people
- environment
- community
- marketplace.

Escobar's use of violence against his opponents provides insight into the benefits of implementing an **Employee Code of Conduct Policy** setting forth the elements of the company's discipline program. A discipline program should outline the penalties imposed for common offences according to the Code of Conduct. Likewise, employee loyalty cannot exist in an environment where superior performance goes unrecognised. An Employee Code of Conduct Policy would provide a company with a consistent way of improving performance of employees by outlining company expectations and rewards.

SUMMARY

Pablo Escobar acquired unprecedented notoriety and power in the Columbian cocaine trade by controlling the distribution chain, adapting his business model to maximise profits, and manipulating the impoverished Medellín community with a Robin Hood persona. Escobar quickly expanded his cocaine empire, using bribes, extortion or violence to successfully silence his opponents. Escobar's decline in power can be attributed to his pursuit of political status and legitimacy. After he obtained a seat in the Columbian Congress, the media began investigating the source of his wealth and publicised Escobar's connections to the drug trade. When the Columbian Government revoked his seat in Congress, Escobar initiated a reign of terror against the politicians, journalists and civilians who exposed his criminal activities. Pressure from the United States Government prompted the Columbian Government to initiate a manhunt for Escobar, which ultimately resulted in his death and the dismantling of the Medellín Cartel.

DAWOOD IBRAHIM
"MUCHCHAD"

6 DAWOOD IBRAHIM

ORIGIN, RISE TO POWER AND CRIMINAL CAREER

Born on 5 December 1955 in Maharashtra, India (part of a community of Konkani Muslims), Dawood Ibrahim is the head of D-Company, India's largest organised crime syndicate, and is touted as one of the world's wealthiest drug Kingpins. He has been nicknamed 'Muchchad', a nod to his abundant moustache.

Ibrahim's criminal interests are wider than illegal drugs; he is on Interpol's wanted list for organised crime and counterfeiting, and is accused of operating a substantial illegal empire in India, Dubai and Pakistan. Accused of having ties with Osama bin Laden, in 2003 the United States declared Ibrahim a 'Specially Designated Global Terrorist', and brought the matter before the United Nations in an attempt to freeze his assets around the world and crack down on his operations.

Early life

Ibrahim commenced his criminal career as a participant in a gang war in Dongri, Mumbai, fighting on the side of Haji Mastan. Ibrahim fought for Mastan against the Pathan gang, who were mostly migrants from Afghanistan. The Pathan gang killed one of Ibrahim's brothers, and Ibrahim sought revenge in one of Mumbai's deadliest gang wars. Ibrahim killed all the members of the Pathan and Surve gangs and, consequently, grew more powerful and dangerous. When Mastan left the gang to enter politics, Ibrahim assumed leadership of Mastan's gang and began to play a major role in India's underworld.

In India, Ibrahim invested in the ship-breaking (or ship demolition) industry, which he used to smuggle arms, explosives and contraband. He also entered the 'hawala' – or money laundering – trade, which transfers money and remittances outside the scrutiny of official agencies.

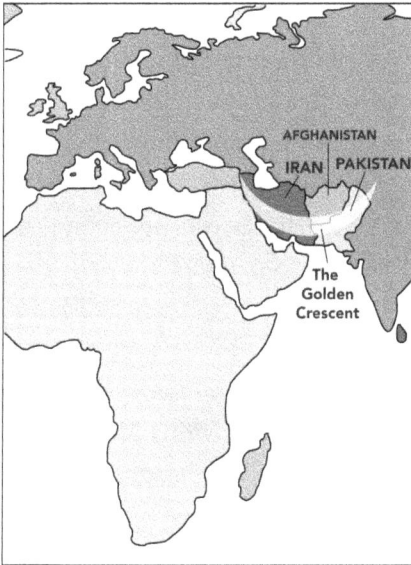

Founded D-Company

In 1986, Ibrahim relocated to Dubai and expanded his business interests. He developed a massive network of both illegal and legal businesses, including a legitimate construction and trading company. His network included both Muslims and Hindus, a diverse group of men typical of the earlier criminal gangs of Mumbai.

Ibrahim's organisation, known as D-Company and 'the Goldman Sachs of Organised Crime', smuggled in drugs, gold, silver, electronic goods and textiles. With a strong network of foot soldiers and lieutenants, accountants, agents, lawyers, corrupt police personnel and judicial officers to manage the gang's legal troubles, D-Company rose to the top of the underworld by the early 1990s.

The real estate industry provided Ibrahim with a golden opportunity to extort protection money from builders and enter into partnerships with them. Ibrahim had a talent for resolving real estate disputes that arose between businessmen.

Ibrahim also built a luxurious mansion in Dubai, where he hosted decadent parties, inviting Mumbai's most famous celebrities, cricketers and politicians. Ibrahim was known as a Muslim boy from Dongri who had successfully taken control of entire criminal enterprises and silenced rival Hindu dons. Muslims in the Mumbai slums looked up to him as an empowering vindicator of the Islamic minority.

Bombay bombings

Ibrahim became radicalised in the 1990s, forging relationships with Islamists, including Laskar e-Toiba and al Qaeda. Ibrahim is also believed to have had contact with al Qaeda leader Osama bin Laden during this time.

In January 1993, widespread rioting took place in Mumbai after militant Hindu nationalist groups destroyed the Babri Masjid mosque in Ayodhya, India. In March 1993, in retaliation for the destruction of the mosque, a series of 13 coordinated bombs were detonated in Bombay, India. The explosions left 257 people dead in what were considered the most destructive bombings in Indian history. Ibrahim was immediately implicated as a key organiser and financer of the Bombay attacks.

Ibrahim's involvement in the Bombay attacks divided D-Company along religious lines. In 1996, Chhota Rajan, one of Ibrahim's main subordinates, formed his own gang in retaliation for the Bombay attacks. Rajan was Hindu, as were most of his own affiliates. A schism developed between the Muslims who stayed with D-Company and the Hindus who left to join Rajan's gang. As a result, more than a hundred men were killed in Mumbai in a series of gang-related homicides.

After Ibrahim became radicalised, conflicting allegiances complicated his role as 'don' of D-Company. The dual nature of the role required Ibrahim to manage the diversity of his successful criminal organisation while he experienced increasing pressure to avenge the Muslim minorities of Mumbai. Ibrahim's decision to coordinate the 1993 terrorist bombings caused permanent damage to his criminal syndicate. The public nature of the Bombay attacks resulted in significant unwanted attention being directed towards D-Company. Sectarian division harmed D-Company's activity after infighting broke out in the late 1990s.

In the late 1990s, Ibrahim travelled in Afghanistan under the Taliban's protection. Ibrahim's participation in the Bombay attacks and ties to the Taliban prompted the United States Department of the Treasury to designate him as a terrorist and include him in its international sanctions program. The program effectively forbids United States financial entities from working with Ibrahim and permits the seizure of assets believed to be under his control.

Drug smuggling operation

The United States reports D-Company operates smuggling routes from South Asia, the Middle East and Africa, and that Ibrahim's syndicate is involved in large-scale shipments of narcotics in the United Kingdom and Western Europe.

After the Bombay bombings, Ibrahim and D-Company went into hiding and their operation ceased all detectable activity. In 1997, Ibrahim purportedly re-emerged as a major player in the global narcotics trade. According to one Indian news source, Ibrahim owed his successful return to the Liberation Tigers of Tamil Eelam (LTTE). The LTTE assisted Ibrahim in transporting narcotics abroad and streamlining D-Company's operations in India through LTTE's bases in the south (the coastal areas of Tuticorin and Thanjavur) and in the west (Mumbai and the creeks of Gujarat). LTTE's network of operations was believed to be so complex – with at least four layers of middlemen who took orders and transported product – that not even a single transaction could be traced to Ibrahim.

The majority of heroin deals were negotiated in Dubai, and the heroin was procured in Karachi and transported across the Gujarat border. Once in Gujarat, the drug was transported to Mumbai, and then abroad via a variety of innovative methods. One technique involved sorting the heroin in 1 to 2 kg waterproof packets and loading the packets into milk trucks or oil tankers. Once near Mumbai, D-Company retrieved the packets from the tankers and distributed the heroin abroad, either through containers in ships or on Mafia boats departing from the coast near Mumbai.

According to underworld sources, the LTTE conducted a training camp for D-Company to teach Ibrahim's men innovative ways of packing heroin. Smuggling heroin in false-bottom suitcases was abandoned for scooping out oranges, filling them with heroin and packing the drug in fruit tin cans. D-Company set up export–import agencies in Mumbai to handle the packaging task.

Ibrahim's younger brother, Anis, acted as Ibrahim's frontman, operating from a spacious office in Deira, Dubai. Anis allegedly took orders by telephone and negotiated deals – subject to Ibrahim's approval – from Karachi. Anis also supervised the India operations in extortion and financing of films and construction in Mumbai.

Recent drug smuggling activity

In July 2014, D-Company reportedly partnered with the al Qaida–controlled terror outfit Boko Haram. An Islamic extremist group based in northeastern Nigeria, Boko Haram means 'western education is a sin'.

Boko Haram sought to exploit D-Company's drug network to smuggle drugs into India. Ibrahim allegedly facilitated the formation of several Boko Haram drug cartels and agreed to act as one of Boko Haram's suppliers.

Recent ties with politicians in real estate projects

In December 2015, an investigation by *The Hindu* newspaper established that in Maharashtra, India, several politicians have long-standing, or newly established, ties with D-Company in the form of a criminal–politician network with significant muscle and money power. The newspaper reported that documents show that over the past few years Ibrahim and his assistant Chhota Shakeel have secretly influenced important redevelopment schemes in South Mumbai through their local political connections. The operators of the project were not aware of the influence being exerted, and the connection between the politicians and D-Company indicates a resurgence of Ibrahim's collective.

It is understood that the influence of politicians has been used by D-Company to both settle matters in redevelopment schemes and also in other developments. Over the past twenty years various allegations and criminal charges been made in relation to this criminal/political nexus. There are, allegedly, a number of politicians who are linked closely with Ibrahim and his team; there are other politicians that have managed to distance themselves from former underworld operatives to now being mainstream politicians.

Ibrahim is currently believed to reside in Karachi, Pakistan, although Pakistan has always denied his presence there.

CAREER HIGHLIGHTS AND LEGAL LESSONS

Dawood Ibrahim's rise to power and career achievements were facilitated by his high business acumen. He developed a network of successful illegal and legal businesses, overcame a rift in D-Company after the Bombay bombings and established a criminal–politician network to facilitate redevelopment projects.

Business growth

In Dubai, Ibrahim built a massive network of successful illegal and legal businesses. He formed D-Company, a criminal enterprise comprising both Muslims and Hindus, which smuggled drugs, precious metals, electronic goods and textiles. Real estate provided Ibrahim with a golden opportunity to extort protection money from builders and enter into partnerships with them. Businessmen often called upon Ibrahim to resolve real estate disputes arising between them.

Ibrahim managed his legal risks via extortion and bribery tactics. Focusing on legal compliance assists legitimate businesses and can be accomplished through the implementation of an **Audit and Compliance Policy**. Such a policy will recognise that compliance risk is inherent in any operation, and commits the company to maintaining a structured and consistent approach to compliance with a view to actively managing compliance risk.

Ibrahim implemented a **Dispute Resolution Policy** to settle disputes between the real estate professionals involved in his partnerships. (A more detailed description of Dispute Resolution Policies are discussed later in the Legal Lessons of Guzmán.)

Ibrahim, whose network included both Muslims and Hindus, implemented a **Diversity Policy**, the benefits of which were discussed in the Legal Lessons of Lucas.

Rift within D-Company after 1993 Bombay bombings

Ibrahim's association with the terrorist attack on Bombay brought unwanted attention to D-Company, causing a rift among his Hindu and Muslim personnel and substantial damage to his criminal syndicate.

In this example, Ibrahim – as the leader of D-Company – was believed to have betrayed some members of his team. The same thing can occur in a company if a leader is seen to have made profits unfairly; for example, by using information they had as a result of their position in an ASX-listed company. One way to avoid this is by implementing a **Securities Trading Policy**, which is separate from and additional to the legal constraints imposed by the common law, the *Corporations Act 2001* (Cth) and the ASX Listing Rules.

A Securities Trading Policy will regulate trading by certain restricted persons in the securities of the company. The policy also sets forth specific periods during which certain persons may not deal in the securities unless an exceptional circumstance applies. Many terms will be specifically defined and there will be a prohibition on insider trading included in the policy.

Criminal–politician network in redevelopment projects

After he appeared on Interpol's wanted list, Ibrahim went into hiding. His presence was recently detected in South Mumbai, where he established a criminal–politician network, using the influence of politicians to facilitate the settlement of redevelopment projects he finances.

A company can benefit by managing its political relationships through a **Government Relations Policy**. In a complex and ever-changing regulatory environment, for some companies it is important to have a strong capacity to anticipate and respond to changes in government policy.

SUMMARY

After assuming leadership of Haji Mastan's former crime gang, Dawood Ibrahim established his position as a major player in India's underworld. He solidified his power by forming D-Company, a sophisticated, diverse criminal network comprising both Hindus and Muslims, and by expanding his illegal and legitimate business interests in Dubai. He developed smuggling routes from South Asia, the Middle East and Africa, and controls large-scale shipments of narcotics in the United Kingdom and Western Europe.

Ibrahim's involvement in the 1993 Bombay bombings established his allegiance to the Muslim minorities in Mumbai, causing a rift in the D-Company organisation, marking him as a terrorist, and forcing him into hiding. Despite the aftermath of the Bombay bombings, which included a temporary interruption of his business operations, Ibrahim has re-emerged in India's underworld. His presence and influence have recently been detected in South Mumbai real estate ventures and a drug smuggling partnership with the al Qaida–controlled Islamic extremist group Boko Haram.

7 JOAQUÍN ARCHIVALDO GUZMÁN LOERAS

ORIGIN AND RISE TO POWER

Born in La Tuna de Badiraguato, Sinaloa, Mexico on 4 April 1957 (although other sources state 25 December 1954), Joaquín Archivaldo Guzmán Loeras, known as 'El Chapo', is a Mexican drug lord and head of Mexico's Sinaloa Cartel. His nickname El Chapo means 'Shorty' in English (he is 5'6" or 168 cm). After the arrest of Guzmán's main rival – Osiel Cárdenas of the Gulf Cartel – in 2003, Guzmán was recognised as Mexico's top drug Kingpin.

From 2009 to 2011, *Forbes* magazine ranked Guzmán as one of the most powerful people in the world, ranking

41st, 60th, and 55th, respectively In 2011, Guzmán was named the 10th richest man in Mexico, with a net worth of roughly US$1 billion. In 2012, the United States Department of the Treasury deemed Guzmán the 'most powerful drug trafficker in the world'. The United States Drug Enforcement Administration (DEA) estimates Guzmán has exceeded the power, influence and achievements of Pablo Escobar and now considers him 'the Godfather of the drug world'.

Early life

Raised in the rural community of La Tuna with his younger brothers and sisters, Guzmán came from a poor and abusive family. His father earned his living as a cattle rancher and possibly an opium poppy farmer.

As a child, Guzmán sold oranges before leaving school in the third grade to cultivate opium poppies with his father. Guzmán and his brothers would hike the hills to harvest and stack the poppies, which his father sold to suppliers in Culiacán and Guamúchil. Guzmán also sold marijuana at commercial centres in the area. At age 15, Guzmán grew his own marijuana and financially supported his family with the earnings from the harvest. His father kicked him out of his house when he was still a teenager, and Guzmán went to live with his grandfather. When he was in his 20s, Guzmán left La Tuna in search of greater opportunities. With the help of his uncle Pedro Avilés Pérez – one of the pioneers of Mexican drug trafficking – Guzmán entered the world of organised crime.

Entry into organised crime

During the 1980s, the leading crime syndicate in Mexico was the Guadalajara Cartel, headed by Miguel Ángel Félix Gallardo. In the 1970s, Guzmán transported drugs and oversaw shipments for the Mexican drug lord Héctor Palma.

The leaders of the Guadalajara Cartel liked Guzmán's business acumen, and in the early 1980s they introduced Guzmán to Félix Gallardo. Gallardo put Guzmán in charge of logistics, and he coordinated drug shipments from Colombia to Mexico by land, air and sea. Palma, on the other hand, made sure the deliveries arrived to consumers in the United States. Guzmán soon earned enough standing to work for Gallardo directly.

Formation of Tijuana, Juárez and Sinaloa cartels

In 1989, Gallardo, the head of the Guadalajara Cartel, was arrested and imprisoned. During his time in prison Gallardo called for a high-level meeting. During the meeting, Gallardo, Guzmán and others agreed to allocate the territories previously claimed by the Guadalajara Cartel. The Arellano Félix brothers formed the Tijuana Cartel; a group controlled by the Carrillo Fuentes family formed the Juárez Cartel; and the remaining faction formed the Sinaloa Cartel, controlled by traffickers Ismael Zambada, Palma and Guzmán.

Exporting to the United States

While exporting drugs to the US, Guzmán practised a strategy of outsourcing all but the most strategic activities. Guzmán's business really took off when he was able to turn the tables on the Columbian cocaine cartel that originally wanted him to get its product into the United States. Miguel Angel Martínez, an independent contractor who was paid a fee by the Colombians to move their cocaine, figured out how to fly it from South America to obscure

Mexican landing strips. This gave Mexico better access to the United States after government officials closed down the Caribbean route Columbia used to export cocaine. When Martinez, working with Guzmán, started getting paid in cocaine, instead of cash, the massive logistical operation that Martinez ran became the most profitable part of the industry.

Guzmán constantly innovated in his core activity, and he was extremely creative when it came to transporting drugs from Mexico into the United States. To that end, the Sinaloa Cartel smuggled cocaine on commercial flights and eventually on its own 747s; used container ships, fishing vessels, go-fast boats and submarines that could be sunk if discovered to hide evidence; dug tunnels between Mexico and the United States; and put drugs in vacuum-sealed cans of chili peppers from a canning factory he purchased.

Guzmán managed his risk compulsively. Among the most significant risks that any Kingpin faces are the risks of being killed or captured, and the potential to lose inventory or not get paid for it. In response to these risks, Guzmán used the following strategies:

- splitting big shipments into smaller ones of, say, five shipments of 20 kilos each
- sharing the investment with partners

- compartmentalising roles of the few who worked for Sinaloa directly
- setting traps for wholesalers and retailers to test their trustworthiness.

When Guzmán was arrested in 2014, it is understood that he had brought more illegal drugs into the United States than any other Kingpin. Guzmán saw an opportunity to benefit from the clampdown on the cartels in Columbia, and during this time he managed to gain business and market share; Columbia's own cartels were destroyed. He took similar advantage when rival cartels were annihilated by a Mexican Government crackdown; his Sinaloa gang came through largely unscathed.

The first tunnel

Guzmán's greatest contribution to the evolving tradecraft of drug trafficking was a tunnel. In the late 1980s, Guzmán hired an architect to design an underground passageway from Mexico to the United States. What appeared to be a water faucet outside the home of a cartel attorney in the border town of Agua Prieta in Mexico was in fact a secret lever that, when twisted, activated a hydraulic system that opened a hidden trapdoor underneath a pool table inside the house. The passage ran more than 200 feet, directly beneath the fortifications along the border, and emerged inside a warehouse the cartel owned in Douglas, Arizona.

When this new route was complete, Guzmán sent a message to the Colombians, requesting they send all the drugs they could. As the deliveries multiplied, the Sinaloa Cartel acquired a reputation for the speed with which it could push inventory across the border. Allegedly, before the planes were arriving back in Colombia on the return, the cocaine was already in Los Angeles.

The tunnel into Douglas, Arizona remains Guzmán's masterpiece, an emblem of his creative ingenuity. Twenty years later, the cartels are still burrowing under the border. More than a hundred tunnels have been discovered in the years since Guzmán's tunnel. They are often ventilated and air-conditioned, and some feature trolley lines stretching up to a half-mile to accommodate the tonnage in transit.

Innovation

Eventually Guzmán's tunnel was discovered, so he shifted tactics by going into the chili-pepper business. Guzmán opened a cannery in Guadalajara and began producing thousands of cans stamped 'Comadre Jalapeños', stuffing them with cocaine, and then vacuum-sealing and shipping them to Mexican-owned grocery stores in California. Guzmán sent drugs in the refrigeration units of tractor-trailers, in custom-made cavities in the bodies of cars and in truckloads of fish. He transported drugs across the border on freight trains to cartel warehouses in Los Angeles and

Chicago, where rail spurs let the cars roll directly inside to unload. He also sent drugs via FedEx.

Conflict with the Tijuana Cartel

Almost immediately following Gallarado's arrest and the formation of the Tijuana, Juarez and Sinaloa cartels, a conflict between the Tijuana and Sinaloa cartels developed. The cartels began killing off each other's associates. In early 1992, a Tijuana Cartel–affiliated and San Diego–based gang kidnapped six of Guzmán's men in Tijuana, tortured them to obtain information, and then shot them in the backs of their heads. Their bodies were dumped on the outskirts of the city. Shortly after the attack, a car bomb exploded outside one of Guzmán's properties in Culiacán. No injuries were reported, but the drug lord became aware the Tijuana Cartel had put a hit on him.

In November 1992, gunmen of Arellano Félix attempted to kill Guzmán as he was driving a vehicle through the streets of Guadalajara, but Guzmán escaped unharmed. The war between the cartels continued for six more months; during this time none of their leaders were killed.

In May 1993, the Tijuana Cartel sent its top gunmen on a final mission to kill Guzmán in Guadalajara, where he moved around frequently to avoid attacks. The hitmen had no success, so they decided to return to Baja California to look for Guzmán there. Before they left Tijuana they received a tip that Guzmán was at the airport in the car park waiting for a flight to Puerto Vallarta. The men found the car that they thought Guzmán was hiding in, and about 20 of them got out of their vehicles and opened fire on it.

Guzmán was inside a different car a short distance away. Cardinal and Archbishop of Guadalajara, Juan Jesús Posadas Ocampo, was inside the target car, and he died at the scene from fourteen gunshot wounds. Guzmán escaped. The death of the Cardinal, who was a highly respected religious figure, caused an outpouring of grief and fury from the Mexican public, the Catholic Church and politicians. A massive manhunt was undertaken to arrest the people involved, including the government offering million-dollar bounties for each of them. Pictures of Guzmán's face started to appear for the first time in newspapers and on television screens across Mexico.

First imprisonment

In June 1993, Guzmán was arrested in Guatemala and extradited to Mexico. Guzmán's sentence was significant: he was sentenced to 20 years and 9 months on charges of drug trafficking, criminal association and bribery. He was transferred to the Federal Centre for Social Rehabilitation No. 2, a maximum security prison also known as 'Puente Grande' in Jalisco, Mexico in 1995.

While he was incarcerated, Guzmán's drug empire was operated under the supervision of his brother, Arturo Guzmán Loera. Despite his imprisonment, Guzmán himself was still considered to be a major international Kingpin by the United States and Mexico. It has been alleged that members of the cartel delivered suitcases of cash that Guzmán used to bribe prison workers. Prison guards reportedly acted as his servants while he upheld his extravagant lifestyle.

First escape

Puente Grande was the toughest prison in Mexico at the time. Each prisoner in the institution was assigned two guards, and the prison had a sophisticated surveillance system to detect any escape attempts. Despite the safeguards, in 2001 Guzmán escaped from the prison. According to a report by the *New York Times*, Guzmán needed a lot of help to escape, and he obtained it by bribing a large number of prison employees. Someone opened his electronically secured cell, disabled the video cameras, smuggled him onto a laundry truck in a burlap bag, and drove him away from the prison.

Second imprisonment

In 2014, Guzmán was recaptured and imprisoned again, this time in Altiplano prison, Mexico's highest security prison.

Second escape

In July 2015, Guzmán escaped from Altiplano prison via a 1.5 kilometre tunnel that started from a secluded section of his cell and ended in an unfinished building located in an open field.

After his second escape, Guzmán's brazen behaviour and careless habits caught the attention of authorities and aided them in tracking his whereabouts. The most damning signs of his carelessness were his sordid relationship with actress Kate del Castillo and his meeting with American actor Sean Penn. Guzmán approached Hollywood producers to pitch a film about his life, soliciting actress Kate del Castillo to coordinate the venture, and granting an interview to Sean Penn in a secret location in Mexico. This is most likely to have stirred Mexican authorities, as it would have been an embarrassment for both the Mexican President and security forces, making them even more determined to catch Guzmán. Had Guzmán been vigilant, he could have enjoyed a longer period of freedom before he was recaptured.

Third imprisonment

In January 2016, Guzmán was recaptured and taken back to Altiplano. This time, security was tightened both in and around the prison to prevent another escape by the drug lord. Some of the measures taken to deter another escape include moving Guzmán to random cells each day, housing him with fewer inmates to reduce confusion in the event of an emergency, and providing light tanks and armoured vehicles stationed right outside the prison to prevent an attack. Further away from the prison, checkpoints also feature extra security personnel and sandbagged areas.

At the time of writing, Guzmán was awaiting extradition to the United States.

CAREER HIGHLIGHTS AND LEGAL LESSONS

Export market

Guzmán focused primarily on the challenge of getting drugs from Mexico across the US border and into the hands of distributors. In exporting drugs to the United States, Guzmán outsourced all but the most strategic activities. He devised new innovations for operating his core activity (drug smuggling) and compulsively managed the risks of his enterprise.

The previously mentioned **Procurement Policy** can benefit a company by addressing the company's commitment to focusing on its special skills while outsourcing activities in which it lacks expertise.

A **Risk Management Policy** can provide guidelines for managing the risk of innovation and other activities. Such a policy serves two main purposes: to identify, reduce and prevent undesirable incidents or outcomes, and to review past incidents and implement changes to prevent or reduce future incidents.

A company that implements a Risk Management Policy adopts a structured and consistent approach to risk management. A Risk Management Policy assists in the alignment of strategy, procedures, people, behaviour and technology for the purpose of evaluating and managing the risks the company faces in creating and protecting shareholder value.

The environment

Guzmán left school in the third grade to cultivate opium poppies with his father. Guzmán and his brothers would hike the hills to harvest and stack the poppies, participating in the process of converting the poppies to raw opium. Guzmán understood first-hand the natural environment his business relied on. The way that Guzmán continued to value the environment was clear in the way he operated as a Kingpin.

An **Environmental Policy** is a statement about an organisation's environmental values, and sets out an organisation's environmental performance intentions and direction. Developing an Environmental Policy can benefit an organisation because it can show that it has considered its environmental impact and has adopted best practice or is working towards improving its environmental performance. It can also provide clear direction to all stakeholders about the organisation's environmental values.

Conflict

Conflict can be harmful to your business and can divert time, energy and money away from its goals. The conflict between the Tijuana and Sinaloa cartels resulted in Guzmán being the target of multiple assassination attempts and the focus of a manhunt for individuals involved in the shootout that killed Cardinal Posadas Ocampo. Guzmán might have avoided his first arrest had he initiated **Dispute Resolution Policies** to end the dispute between the Tijuana and Sinaloa cartels. Guzmán was working with a different set of risks in this area of course.

A company can benefit from implementing an internal Dispute Resolution Policy to help it decide when and when not to take action to settle a dispute. Dispute-related organisational policies when properly implemented will:

- set out internal structures, process and protocols
- delegate authority at various levels (for example, to negotiate, agree, settle)
- confirm the organisation's attitude towards the resolution of disputes (for example, aggressive, non-confrontational)

- set out the materiality thresholds
- confirm preferences regarding giving of undertakings, indemnities, warranties
- set out compliance programs and registers.

As we have seen with many of the Kingpins, the impacts of disputes on an organisation can be significant, and can include:

- board of management time wasted and distraction from the business
- adverse publicity and/or shareholder anxiety
- potential liability for damages and costs if litigation occurs
- fees of external lawyers and other advisors or experts
- disruption to day-to-day business operations – especially if there is an injunction.

Imprisonment

Guzmán escaped twice from Mexican prisons. After escaping, he was arrogant, complacent and careless. Oftentimes he employed violence to achieve the status of legend, which consequently brought him more negative attention. The attention worked against Guzmán, as authorities became hungrier to capture him, mostly in order to save face. To manage the risk to his health and safety of recapture, Guzmán would have benefited from the implementation of a **Work Health and Safety Policy**.

Leaders of companies are responsible and at risk of personal liability/imprisonment for breaches of occupational health and safety legislation. Implementing a Work Health and Safety Policy will confirm that your company is committed to the health and safety of all employees in the workplace and aims to promote and maintain the physical and mental health of all employees. Such a policy will also confirm that employees do have a responsibility to promote and protect their own safety and that of others in the workplace. The policy will also confirm the company's commitment to remove or reduce potential risks to the health, safety and welfare of all workers, contractors and visitors.

Innovation

Guzmán's greatest contribution to the evolving tradecraft of drug trafficking was an underground passageway from Mexico to the United States. In addition, Guzmán hired an architect to design and build an elaborate tunnel to facilitate his prison break.

Eventually Guzmán's tunnel to the United States was discovered, so he devised new smuggling tactics, including shipping drugs in cans of chilli peppers, the refrigeration units of tractor-trailers, custom-made cavities in the bodies of cars and truckloads of fish.

Innovation within a legitimate business is often associated with the introduction of new products or services; however, it can also be about changing the way you do business. Innovation embraces new uses of technologies, improved industry methods, meeting changing customer demands or needs, and better systems and processes. To be successful, innovation will need to be supported by you, your staff and all other business partners.

When a business develops a focus on innovation it will ensure everyone in the business is working towards better business practices and improving business efficiency and performance. There are some other benefits, including:

- increased competitiveness – higher efficiency with lower costs and higher quality products

- more efficient use of all resources

- improved staff retention – staff like to work in innovative and challenging jobs that promote teamwork and problem solving

- proactive approach to business – your business model is continually matching changing conditions

- greater attraction of new customers by improving existing, or offering new, products or services or entering new markets.

A company's approach to innovation will be driven by the business strategy, capability, market understanding and commitment to the process. These processes can often add a new dimension to your business with little or no additional costs, but with great benefit because a business's ability to compete and survive is directly linked to its ability to innovate.

Guzmán is certainly an innovator, but in business your employees are one of your most productive assets. Encouraging an environment of innovation within a business can create a business that inspires team members to share their knowledge, ideas, experience, skills, recommendations and suggestions.

In addition to creating and implementing an **Innovation Process** within your business, providing clear guidelines for assessing each new idea, ensure that employees are encouraged to make suggestions and recommendations so that they can be confident that the idea will be appropriately considered. Timely acknowledgment and feedback are important aspects of the process to also consider.

Training is also an important aspect of fostering innovation within a business, offering training to employees that will inspire new thoughts and approaches to the business. A **Training and Development Policy** can be of use to acknowledge that team members already bring a range of knowledge, experience and skills when they are employed, but this can be enhanced with specific knowledge relevant to the role and responsibilities of employees.

The policy could recognise that training needs should be identified through a range of inputs, including a training needs assessment and the annual assessment of employee performance, and a training program developed that addresses the knowledge gaps identified. Once identified, the training program should be designed so it provides for individual employee training as well as providing group training opportunities.

SUMMARY

Guzmán's rise to power can be attributed to an ability to specialise and innovate. He specialised in exporting drugs to the United States, outsourcing the remaining tasks of distribution. In addition, Guzmán focused on designing and building underground passageways, not only to export his products from Mexico to the United States, but also to facilitate his escape from a Mexican prison and avoid recapture. Guzmán maintained his wealth and power with innovation. After discovery of his Mexico–United States tunnel, he developed a variety of new methods to transport his products over the United States border, including shipping drugs in cans of chilli peppers, the refrigeration units of tractor-trailers, custom-made cavities in the bodies of cars, and truckloads of fish.

Despite his enormous success in the drug trade, Guzmán never resolved the disputes that created constant conflict with rival cartels. The violent conflict with the Tijuana Cartel disrupted the operation of Guzmán's drug enterprise and led to his first arrest, public recognition, conviction and imprisonment. After his first escape from prison, Guzmán became arrogant, complacent and careless, and he was recaptured and imprisoned again. Although he escaped once more, the Mexican authorities easily tracked, located and recaptured Guzmán. Now awaiting extradition to the United States, Guzmán's continued dominance of the Mexican drug trade seems unlikely.

8 CHRISTOPHER COKE ('DUDUS')

ORIGIN AND RISE TO POWER

Born in Kingston, Jamaica on 13 March 1969, Christopher Coke (also known as 'The President' and 'Dudus') is a Jamaican drug and weapons smuggler and head of the Shower Posse, a vicious Jamaican crime organisation that exported substantial amounts of cocaine and marijuana into Canada, the United States, the Caribbean and the United Kingdom.

Early life

Coke was the adopted son of Lester Coke, a key enforcer for Jamaica's former Prime Minister Edward Seaga, leader of the Jamaica Labour Party, and a co-founder and leader of the Shower Posse. Due to his powerful connections with Prime Minister Seaga, Coke's father could commit crimes with immunity.

With the United States as his biggest market, Coke's father acquired tremendous power and wealth in the 1980s. Despite being the leader of a violent syndicate that trafficked drugs globally, Lester Coke spent most of his time with his family in Kingston, enjoying his riches and power in relative peace and quiet.

Coke and his siblings were raised in a wealthy household and attended expensive private schools with children of Jamaica's political elite. Coke's father succeeded in giving his children a more affluent life than the one he had growing up in the Kingston ghetto, but he also exposed them to the brutal violence of his drug enterprise, a business that would eventually cost him his own freedom and life, as well as the lives of two of his children.

Formation of the Shower Posse

Coke's father and his friend Vivian Blake formed the Shower Posse in the 1980s. As co-leaders of the organisation, Blake was responsible for the US-based operations while Coke's father handled the Jamaican side of the business.

As the Shower Posse extended its drug network to several major cities in the United States it attracted the attention of American authorities, who grew concerned over an increase in gruesome violence connected to the Jamaican drug traffickers.

In 1987, Coke's sister Mumpi was shot and killed during a gunfight with rivals of the Shower Posse. Mumpi was reportedly crying over her boyfriend's dead body when his killers walked up to her and ended her life as well.

In 1990, the United States Department of Justice indicted Coke's father and several other key members of the Shower Posse on federal drug and murder charges. Coke's father was arrested by Jamaican authorities. As he sat in a Jamaican prison awaiting an extradition trial, Coke's older brother, Mark 'Jah T' Coke, was shot off his motorbike and killed. Shortly thereafter, Coke's father died in a mysterious prison fire.

Coke's rise to power

After his father's death when Coke was 23, Coke inherited a dual role as leader of both the Shower Posse and the Tivoli Gardens community. Coke fought off and defeated ambitious rival gangs hoping to take advantage of the recent change in leadership.

The Tivoli Gardens community had a history of extreme poverty, and Coke created employment and developed community programs to help the children and other community members. Residents went to Coke for tuition, legal aid, business loans, food and medicine. Coke had so much local support that Jamaican police were unable to enter Tivoli Gardens without the community's consent.

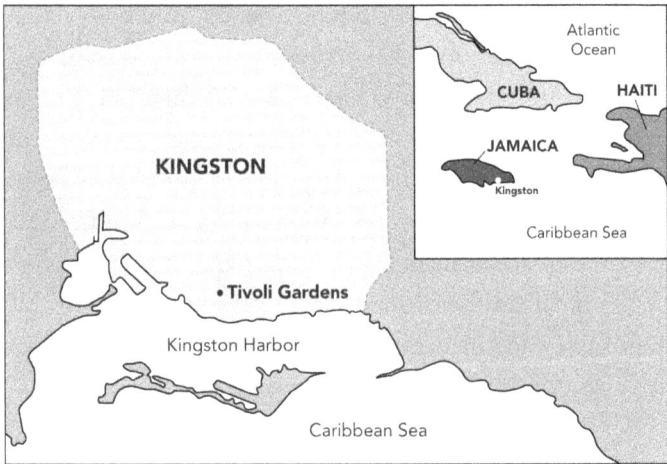

Just like his father before him, Coke received protection from the Jamaican Labour Party, now run by the new Prime Minister, Bruce Golding.

As Coke consolidated his power, his father's death appeared to have little impact on the continued success of the Shower Posse. Drug shipments to the United States continued as they had in the past, and American guns and money were supplied to the Shower Posse.

According to Coke's indictment, beginning in 1994 the Shower Posse sold drugs globally, by the ton. It has been estimated by one investigator that the gang had trafficked into the United States no less than 2,200 pounds of marijuana and almost as much cocaine. Coke also smuggled drugs into the United Kingdom and Canada.

Acquisition of firearms from the United States

A significant factor contributing to Coke's rise to power involved the acquisition of firearms. The Shower Posse made significant investments in firearms obtained primarily from the United States. The firearms were critical not only to Coke's ability to control and strengthen his organisation, but also to maintain his own power within it.

Shower Posse 'soldiers' personally received firearms issued to them by Coke, and followed a Code of Conduct for their use. The soldiers were responsible for maintaining control over their firearms – loss of a firearm could result in serious penalties, including death. Soldiers were required to use their firearms only in accordance with the directions of Coke and his lieutenants. The soldiers' responsibilities included: guarding narcotics in stash houses within or outside Tivoli Gardens; defending the area against rival organisations; locating, apprehending and in some cases punishing individuals at Coke's direction; and participating in election-related activities, including 'motivating' members of surrounding communities to support particular candidates by intimidation.

Coke's acquisition of firearms allowed him to maintain strict order and discipline within the Tivoli Gardens community. For example, the soldiers' easy access to fire-arms rendered the Tivoli Gardens area virtually off-limits to the local police. As a result, Coke resolved all allegations of criminal conduct by or among organisation members. Coke served as fact-finder with respect to allegations of wrongdoing, and he set and directed the imposition of the appropriate punishment. Coke also enforced rules governing the Shower Posse's conduct. No-one could possess or use a firearm, sell cocaine or commit robberies within Tivoli Gardens or the surrounding communities without Coke's authorisation.

COMMUNITY LEADERSHIP

Coke was the government in the Tivoli Gardens com-munity. He was the people's provider and protector where the politicians and police had failed. Under circumstances where the Jamaican Government seemed powerless or unwilling to provide a safety net for the poor, leaders of criminal organisations often stepped in to catch the people who fell through. To the members of the Tivoli Gardens community, Coke was not just the head of a criminal organisation, he was a community leader.

Before his arrest and extradition to the United States in 2010, Coke lived a luxurious lifestyle, spending lavishly at social events and – based on the word of residents of West Kingston – giving generously to those around him. Publicly, his company Presidential Click staged a number of successful stage shows, parties and adults' and children's events. Coke was also a director of Incomparable Enterprise, a company that received lucrative government and private contracts.

US indictment

In August 2009, US authorities charged Coke with organising marijuana and crack cocaine deals, and funnelling the profits, along with weapons, back to Jamaica. The United States requested that the Jamaican Government extradite Coke on drug trafficking and weapons charges. Prime Minister Golding, leader of the Labour Party, initially refused to extradite Coke. He claimed the United States wiretapped (eavesdropped) without a warrant and improperly obtained its evidence against Coke.

In early May 2010, Golding relented and agreed to aid US efforts to extradite Coke. The Jamaican Government issued a warrant for Coke's arrest. After learning of the news, Coke's supporters allegedly began protesting and arming themselves in the Tivoli Gardens community.

Tivoli Gardens massacre

In late May 2010, the national government placed Kingston under a state of emergency when a series of shootings and fire bombings occurred within the city. Jamaican military and police forces then launched a large-scale operation in Kingston to enter Tivoli Gardens and arrest Coke. At least 76 people were killed in clashes between Jamaican security forces and gunmen in West Kingston, primarily in the neighbourhood of Tivoli Gardens.

Following the tragedy, the Jamaican people called for an investigation into the massacre, questioning whether the main reason for the 'incursion' was to arrest Coke or to dismantle the perceived insurgency within the Tivoli Gardens community.

One analyst concluded that the Tivoli incursion and subsequent massacre of civilians was based on a counterinsurgency doctrine most likely formulated by Jamaica's Military Intelligence Unit. The analyst opined that the Jamaican Government declared war on Tivoli Gardens and the wider area of West Kingston, and that no distinction was made between armed combatants and the civilian population in the attack on Tivoli Gardens. It was also alleged that the threat to the Jamaican Government posed by gunmen loyal to Coke was greatly exaggerated and used as a pretext to carry out the planned counterinsurgency operation.

Surrender, extradition and sentencing

Coke said his decision to surrender was based on a desire to end the drug-related violence in Jamaica, to which he'd already lost his sister, brother and father. Coke, who believed his life would be endangered if he turned himself over to the police, asked Reverend Al Miller, an influential evangelical priest, to accompany him and facilitate the surrender.

On 22 June 2010, on his way to surrender at the United States Embassy in Kingston, Coke was detained during a routine roadblock. Coke voluntarily waived his right to an extradition trial in Jamaica and requested immediate extradition to the United States. The police feared an attack by his supporters, and heavily guarded Coke while he was in custody awaiting extradition.

In 2011, Coke appeared in the New York District Court and pleaded guilty to federal racketeering charges related to drug trafficking and assault. In 2012, he was sentenced to 23 years in federal prison.

CAREER HIGHLIGHTS AND LEGAL LESSONS

Two significant factors contributing to Coke's rise to power were his role as a community leader and the acquisition of firearms from the United States.

Community leadership

In Tivoli Gardens, Coke's role as a community leader overshadowed his nefarious involvement with the Shower Posse. Coke took better care of his community than the average business person or politician. He acted as the people's provider and protector where politicians and police had failed, distributing money to the area's poor, creating employment, and setting up community centres to help children and seniors. Coke ultimately surrendered to authorities to end the violence that allegedly erupted when his supporters protested the warrant for his arrest issued by the Jamaican Government.

Coke earned the respect and loyalty of his community by implementing policies of social responsibility.

Companies can benefit by implementing a **Corporate Social Responsibility Policy**, which functions as a self-regulatory mechanism whereby a business monitors and ensures its active compliance with the spirit of the law, ethical standards and national or international norms. A Corporate Social Responsibility Policy aims to increase long-term profits and shareholder trust through positive public relations and high ethical standards, thus reducing business and legal risk by taking responsibility for corporate actions.

Coke was excellent at keeping all of his stake-holders informed, and a company may also benefit from implementing a **Shareholder Communication Policy**, which ensures shareholders are provided with ready, equal and timely access to balanced and understandable information about the company (including its financial performance, strategic goals and plans, material developments, governance and risk profile) to enable shareholders to exercise their rights in an informed manner.

Acquisition of firearms from the United States

Acquiring firearms was critical not only to Coke's ability to control and strengthen his organisation, but also to maintain his own power within it. Shower Posse 'soldiers' personally received firearms issued to them by Coke and followed a Code of Conduct concerning their use. Coke understood the importance of regulating the use of firearms and implemented policies to protect himself and the community from the risks they posed.

A parallel lesson for companies involves understanding the importance of protecting IT assets, including hardware and software. A company can protect itself from misuse of company IT assets, potentially caused by careless employees, by implementing a **Hardware and Software Policy**. In most organisations, employees are provided with the use of computer equipment and software programs for the purpose of carrying out their work. Having a Hardware and Software Policy that requires that employees use company hardware and software in a manner that is consistent with agreed guidelines together with other policies, like an **Email and Internet Policy**, **Social Media Policy** and relevant policies within the **Employee Code of Conduct**, can help to protect your company and also the employees.

Tivoli Gardens massacre

Coke failed to protect the Tivoli Gardens community from risks posed by the Jamaican Government's execution of a warrant for his arrest. Coke's supporters allegedly staged a protest and armed themselves in response to news of the warrant. Jamaican military and police forces launched a large-scale operation to enter the neighbourhood of Tivoli Gardens and arrest Coke. At least 76 people were killed in clashes between Jamaican security forces and members of the Tivoli Gardens community.

After the arrest warrant was issued, Coke did not take any precautions to safeguard the wellbeing of the Tivoli Gardens community. Companies, however, can protect their employees from workplace hazards by implementing a **Work Health and Safety Policy**. A primary goal of a workplace safety policy is to establish the expectation that it is the responsibility of all personnel to create and maintain a safe work environment.

SUMMARY

At the age of 23, Coke inherited leadership of the Shower Posse crime organisation. Avoiding the limelight, Coke focused on expanding his drug enterprise's global reach while cultivating support and loyalty from the Tivoli Gardens community. Ruling with a strategic combination of violence, corruption and philanthropy, at the height of his power Coke smuggled tons of marijuana and cocaine into Canada, the United States, the Caribbean and the United Kingdom.

Coke's dominance in the Jamaican drug trade can be attributed to his acquisition of firearms, political connections, and his reputation as a community leader. Importing firearms from the United States enabled Coke not only to control and strengthen his organisation, but also to maintain his own power within it. In exchange for votes, the Prime Minster of the Jamaican Labour Party protected Coke from criminal prosecution. Coke earned the support and loyalty of the Tivoli Gardens community, who were recipients of donations and social programs, neighbourhood security and jobs available through Coke's legitimate businesses.

Coke's downfall can be traced to a failure to lead. Despite his reputation as provider and protector, Coke failed to safeguard his community from the violence that ensued when Jamaican law enforcement and military forces forcibly entered Tivoli Gardens to arrest Coke on US drug and weapons charges. Many were killed in clashes between Jamaican security forces and citizens of Tivoli Gardens, a tragedy later known as the 'Tivoli Gardens massacre'. On his way to surrender to authorities, Coke was nowhere near Tivoli Gardens when Jamaican security forces stormed the community. After his surrender, Coke was extradited to the United States. He pleaded guilty to federal racketeering charges for drug trafficking and assault. In 2012, he started serving a 23-year federal prison term.

9 ROSS WILLIAM ULBRICHT

THE DREAD PIRATE ROBERTS AND SILK ROAD

Origin and notoriety

Ross William Ulbricht was born on 27 March 1984 in Austin Texas.

From a young age he was described as socially curious, kind, helpful and resourceful. He joined the Boy Scouts and got to the rank of Eagle Scout just like his father had. After school, Ulbricht earned a full scholarship to study physics at the University of Texas in Dallas. He fell in love at university, and at his graduation in 2006 he proposed to his girlfriend, but it was not to be. Ulbricht returned to his hometown and tried to figure out what to do with his life.

He applied for a Master's degree at Pennsylvania State University and once again he got a full scholarship. His focus was on Science and Engineering. Up to that point, Ulbricht was deeply interested in mathematics, science and nature, but at Penn State his interest shifted dramatically to the subject of libertarian economic theory. He joined groups to discuss the subject matter and also attended debates on the subject.

After graduating from university, Ulbricht decided that he had no interest in pursuing a career in science – what he wanted to do was become an entrepreneur and develop his own business.

In 2009 Ulbricht wondered if he could create his free trade market idea on the internet and make it untraceable, outside of the control and regulations of the government. It was two years later, in 2011 when he moved to San Francisco, the place so many innovative trailblazing organisations have started, that he launched his business – an online black marketplace called the Silk Road.

Ulbricht's passion for libertarian economics was the foundation for the website, where he called himself the 'Dread Pirate Roberts' and used the dark web, traded only in bitcoin and attempted to evade authorities, who eventually caught up with him.

He was sentenced to life in prison in 2015. His 2017 appeal was denied by the US Court of Appeals. Ulbricht continues to serve a life sentence without parole.

Career highlights and legal lessons

Ulbricht's business, the Silk Road, experienced explosive growth. Ulbricht's initial marketing strategy was to post in online discussion forums, with a view to bringing traffic to the Silk Road. Ulbricht posted in a forum thread on a discussion about using bitcoin to buy and sell heroin and one about magic mushrooms. These two forum posts attracted people to Silk Road on its opening day. No-one bought anything that first day, but it didn't take long before people started buying from the site. Arguably what brought about the first burst of growth in the site was an online media article.

Public relations

On 1 June 2011, an article by journalist Adrian Chen was published on Gawker.com. The title of the article was 'The Underground Website Where You Can Buy Any Drug Imaginable'. The article included photos of the various drugs available in screenshots of the website itself. It was read by millions, and it was this article that brought Silk Road to the masses. At the time of writing, the article was still online here: http://gawker.com/the-underground-website-where-you-can-buy-any-drug-lmag-30818160

What Ulbricht did exceptionally well was focusing on being different from his competitors, rather than being better than them. Being different attracts more interest in what you are doing for less effort. If Ulbricht had built a policy around this point of difference it could have been an **Innovation Policy**. He was learning from organisations that Silk Road existed in parallel to – like Amazon and Facebook.

Home delivery

By creating an online market place, Ulbricht innovated services that had not been achieved by any Kingpin before. One of these innovations, and one of the biggest breakthroughs Silk Road achieved, was enabling people to have drugs delivered to their home, just like any other online purchase.

The sellers all had different methods of hiding their goods, to try to avoid detection by the authorities. Some were much better at it than others! The authorities had red flags for packages: they looked for typed address labels on personal mail and they also looked for a bundle of similar envelopes heading to different addresses with slightly different return addresses.

When Ulbricht started Silk Road, he was growing and selling magic mushrooms. Ulbricht's method for posting his magic mushrooms was to first wrap them up in a plastic Ziploc bag. He then used a second wrapping from the Good Wagon books online store (his other occupation). So the drug delivery was disguised as a book. Lastly he printed out the name and address of the buyer rather than handwriting it. He believed this would look more businesslike and professional and thus would attract less attention.

The business lesson from the home delivery service offered by the Silk Road is that the more your organisation's user experience mirrors an experience your customer is already familiar with, the more likely they are to try your product. Policies that focus on putting your customers or clients first can put you way ahead of your competition – always remember, without customers or clients you do not have a business.

Anonymity

The Silk Road remained hidden from casual internet users for years because it was built on something called the dark web. Building the Silk Road on the dark web was a groundbreaking innovation because it allowed existing distributors to distribute direct to anonymous customers instead of the personal peer-to-peer networks that are the standard distribution method in this industry. This allowed a new category of distributor that was not subject to the normal restrictions placed on them by wholesalers to emerge very quickly.

The dark web

The dark web is an anonymous online space, or series of encrypted networks, which are only accessible with specific software that hides your identity and location. It is not difficult to access this encrypted network. All it takes is downloading darknet software. The most common dark web networks are Tor, I2P, and Freenet.

The Silk Road was accessible by downloading Tor. Tor stands for 'the onion routing project'. It was developed by the US Navy for the government in the mid-1990s. But it was open-sourced in 2004, and that's when it went public. Tor is now the dark web browser that the vast majority of people use to anonymously surf the internet.

Bitcoin

Bitcoin is a crypto-currency (which means it is a form of digital currency created and held electronically) that was created in 2009 by an unknown person using the alias Satoshi Nakamoto. Bitcoin can be used to book hotels, shop for furniture and buy Xbox games. There are no banks needed for bitcoin transactions and international payments are easy and cheap because bitcoins are decentralised, which means no single institution or country controls it, and it's not subject to transaction fees or external regulation.

Though each bitcoin transaction is recorded in a public log, names of buyers and sellers are never revealed – only their wallet IDs. While that keeps bitcoin users' transactions private, it also lets them buy or sell anything without easily tracing it back to them. That's why it has become the currency of choice for people online buying drugs and weapons or engaging in other illicit activities.

The lesson in this is that creating platforms that allow your supply side to operate with less industry regulation will be welcomed by new players and resisted strongly by industry incumbents. Remember to plan for any responses from incumbent players before executing a disruptive technology.

In case of emergency checklist

Ulbricht knew he was playing a dangerous game; he contemplated and prepared for a life on the run.

One file found on Ulbricht's computer was labelled 'Emergency', and contained a list of apparent to-do items in the event that either Ulbricht had learned that law enforcement was closing in on him, or there was another reason he thought it was time to call it a day with the Silk Road.

It reads as follows:

Encrypt and backup important files on laptop to
memory stick
Destroy laptop hard drive and hide/dispose
Destroy phone and hide/dispose
Hide memory stick
Get new laptop
Go to end of train
Find place to live on craigslist for cash
Create new identity (name, backstory)

Have a clear written policy for the known risks that exist
as a result of your business model, industry trends or
legislative environment, and ensure that you are taking
data frequently enough to enact these policies if your
circumstances change.

Using the mail system

Home delivery was an innovation – there is no doubt many
Silk Road sellers chose to use the US postal system. As with
all businesses there are risks and rewards with all decisions
we make.

At one time a Customs and Border Protection officer
came across a small envelope that had the name and address
printed from a computer. Ulbricht had always believed that
printing names and addresses from a computer looked more

businesslike and less suspicious than handwriting them. But on this occasion it was actually the reason the Border Protection officer thought the envelope looked suspicious. The envelope was very small, and normally envelopes of that size had their name and address handwritten. That's what caught the officer's attention initially, but he then saw that the envelope came from the Netherlands, a country known for drug use. Lastly when he felt the envelope he felt a small bump. He filed a report that authorised him to open the envelope and inside he found a pink ecstasy pill.

The lesson in this is that when you're outsourcing an essential yet non-core step in your operations ensure that you design your internal systems to fit snugly with the existing system used by the team you are outsourcing to.

Bugs in the site

Ulbricht was inexperienced building websites; he had never done programming or coding before he built the Silk Road. He realised early on that there were security problems with the site that had to be fixed. When he realised his computer skills were not up to scratch, Ulbricht engaged experts to assist him.

Following this, a Silk Road customer posted on a Reddit forum that something was wrong with Tor's configuration and was showing the actual physical IP address of the server, a post the FBI saw. Before Ulbricht could correct the error, the FBI had tracked down the IP address and found it on a map. Silk Road's server was located in Iceland. The FBI took a trip to the data centre Ulbricht had rented and copied the server's hard disk without Ulbricht suspecting a thing. The FBI didn't know who owned the server yet, so they let Silk Road keep running unchecked.

The lesson? Ensuring that you have robust processes for protecting your intellectual property, especially when working with independent contractors, is paramount. Written contracts that protect your business as best as you possibly can will be absolutely worth the investment.

Security

Ulbricht was first connected to 'Dread Pirate Roberts' by Gary Alford, an IRS investigator working with the DEA on the Silk Road case, in mid-2013. The connection was made by linking the username 'altoid', used during Silk Road's early days to announce the website, and a forum post in which Ulbricht, posting under the nickname 'altoid', asked for programming help and gave his email address, which contained his full name.

When Gary found the email address, he Googled Ulbricht and found his LinkedIn account. He found that Ulbricht was white and from the suburbs but he didn't have a computer science background. Ulbricht had been a physicist. Gary was far from convinced that Ulbricht could be the Dread Pirate Roberts, but he still added him to his suspect list.

This is ultimately what led to Ulbricht's downfall, and the lesson is to ensure you have a clear and agile process for protecting access to your communication systems. Policies and Procedures to keep the most sensitive information confidential are paramount whether you are operating an illegal online marketplace or an ordinary, above board business.

SUMMARY

Ulbricht is now serving a life sentence without parole. Passionate about privacy and free markets, he was 26 years old when he created the site. Silk Road was an online marketplace with an emphasis on user privacy. Using the crypto-currency bitcoin on the Tor browser, people anonymously exchanged a variety of goods.

Silk Road was an illegal trading venture that had a cash flow of at least $213 million, and at the time of his arrest, Ulbricht was believed to be worth $104 million in USD and $20 million in bitcoin. The Silk Road had reportedly handled $9 billion in transactions.

The most important lesson from this modern-day Kingpin is that every action on the internet leaves a trace and, at some point, every criminal will make a mistake.

10 THE TOP 7 REASONS KINGPINS SUCCEED

This book chronologically analyses the business operations of eight notorious and successful drug Kingpins: Frank Lucas (United States), Khun Sa (Mynamar), Griselda Blanco (Columbia), Pablo Escobar (Columbia), Dawood Ibrahim (India), Joaquín Guzmán (Mexico), Christopher Coke (Jamaica) and Ross William Ulbricht (United States). Summaries of the Kingpin's careers are provided below to facilitate an understanding of the conclusion, consisting of a comparative analysis of the drug traffickers' business practices and the lessons learned from their rise and fall from power. There are seven discernible reasons why the Kingpins succeed, and there are lessons the corporate world can learn from these.

1. THEY CAN SELL AND THEY KNOW CUSTOMER SERVICE: FRANK LUCAS (UNITED STATES)

Frank Lucas established his presence in the New York drug trade by breaking up the Italian Mafia's monopoly over heroin supplied to Harlem. His confidence was a blend of attitude and acumen. He travelled to the Golden Triangle and established, developed and protected a wholesale source of raw opium processed into heroin. Lucas managed risks with organisation and oversight, implementing innovative smuggling and customer service strategies that guaranteed the continued success of his enterprise. One flaw in his operation concerned his failure to delegate the financial aspects of the business, an error which ultimately led to his arrest, conviction and the end of his reign in Harlem.

2. THEY KNOW THAT IT'S ALL ABOUT THE PRODUCT: KHUN SA (MYANMAR)

Khun Sa's rise to power in the Golden Triangle opium trade can be attributed to his skill in developing and commanding a sophisticated army to focus on what he knew was most important: the product. Funded by illegal opium profits, Sa's army protected his drug operation and eliminated competition. Sa manipulated and maximised his resources to develop and sustain his army, shifting alliances whenever necessary to acquire an advantage within the opium trade. Sa's decline in power can be attributed to a lack of vision and poor leadership. His professed allegiance to the Shan State brought him into simultaneous conflict with Burma, Thailand, China and the United States, who joined forces to cut off his opium supply line. As Sa's opium network disintegrated, the Shan people began to doubt his commitment to their cause. Despite the loss of his lucrative opium empire, Sa succeeded in avoiding arrest and extradition after he surrendered to the Myanmar Government.

3. IN THE FACE OF COMPETITION, THEY PERSEVERE: GRISELDA BLANCO (COLUMBIA)

Griselda Blanco will be remembered as a ruthless Columbian cocaine trafficker and key member of the Medellín Cartel. Blanco consistently persevered and adhered to her own Code of Conduct advocating violence and intimidation. Despite her fugitive status following an indictment on drug charges in New York, Blanco relocated to Miami, where she continued to expand her distribution network and increase her share of the US cocaine market. Blanco dominated the Miami cocaine scene by killing off her rivals. She flew under the radar of law enforcement by sustaining employee loyalty, and continued to operate her vast cocaine empire even after she was sentenced to prison.

Blanco accumulated a substantial number of enemies in Miami, many of whom actively sought to avenge the deaths of relatives killed by Blanco. Excessive cocaine use fuelled Blanco's paranoia, instability and loss of control. Blanco was the target of so many assassination attempts that she eventually could not leave her Miami mansion without fear of execution. Blanco was forced to relocate to California, a decision which ultimately led to her arrest and contributed to her fall from power in the cocaine underworld.

4. THEY ARE LASER-FOCUSED ON THE BOTTOM LINE: PABLO ESCOBAR (COLUMBIA)

Pablo Escobar acquired unprecedented notoriety and power in the Columbian cocaine trade by controlling the distribution chain, adapting his business model to maximise profits, and manipulating the impoverished Medellín community with a Robin Hood persona. Escobar quickly expanded his cocaine empire, using bribes, extortion and/or violence to successfully silence his opponents. During the height of Escobar's power, the Medellín Cartel earned more than US$70 million per day and smuggled fifteen tons of cocaine per day into the United States.

Escobar's decline in power can be attributed to his pursuit of political status and legitimacy. After he obtained a seat in the Columbian Congress, the media investigated the source of Escobar's wealth and publicised his connections to the drug trade. When the Columbian Government revoked his congressional seat, Escobar initiated a reign of terror, kidnapping and killing several of the politicians, journalists and civilians who exposed his ties to crime. Escobar's violence outraged the Columbian authorities and public. Although he successfully negotiated his surrender in exchange for lenient treatment, the Columbian Government soon discovered Escobar was operating his drug enterprise from prison. Escobar escaped from custody and went into hiding, but Columbia initiated a manhunt. After the United States joined the effort, Escobar was ultimately tracked down and killed while trying to avoid capture, marking the end of Escobar's dominance in the cocaine trade and the dismantling of the Medellín Cartel.

5. THEY KNOW HOW TO INSPIRE PEOPLE: DAWOOD IBRAHIM (INDIA)

After assuming leadership of Haji Mastan's former crime gang, Dawood Ibrahim established his position as a major player in India's underworld. He solidified his power by inspiring people to follow him, and he established D-Company, a sophisticated, diverse criminal network comprising both Hindus and Muslims. He expanded his illegal and legitimate business interests in Dubai, developed smuggling routes from South Asia, the Middle East and Africa, and controlled large-scale shipments of narcotics in the United Kingdom and Western Europe.

Ibrahim's decline in power is linked to his involvement in the 1993 Bombay bombings. His participation in the bombings established his allegiance to the Muslim minorities in Mumbai, caused a rift in the D-Company organisation, marked him as a terrorist, and forced him into hiding.

Despite the aftermath of the Bombay bombings, which included a temporary interruption of his business operations, Ibrahim has re-emerged in India's underworld. His presence and influence have recently been detected in South Mumbai real estate ventures and a drug smuggling partnership with the al Qaida–controlled Islamic extremist group Boko Haram.

6. THEY ARE CUTTING-EDGE INNOVATORS: JOAQUÍN GUZMÁN (MEXICO)

Joaquín Guzmán's rise to power can be attributed to his ability to specialise and innovate. He focused on exporting drugs to the United States and outsourced the remaining tasks of distribution. Guzmán was an expert in designing and building underground passageways, not only to export his products from Mexico to the United States but also to facilitate his escape from prison and to avoid recapture. Guzmán maintained his wealth and power with innovation. After discovery of his Mexico–United States tunnel, he developed a variety of new methods to transport his products over the United States border, including shipping drugs in cans of chilli peppers, the refrigeration units of tractor-trailers, custom-made cavities in the bodies of cars, and truckloads of fish.

Despite his enormous success in the drug trade, Guzmán failed to address or resolve disputes arising between the rival cartels, which ultimately escalated into extreme violence. Guzmán's violent conflict with the Tijuana Cartel disrupted his drug enterprise and prompted a manhunt, leading to his first arrest, subsequent public recognition, conviction and imprisonment. After his first escape from prison, Guzmán became arrogant, complacent and careless, and these qualities facilitated his recapture. After he escaped from prison a second time, Guzmán contacted Hollywood producers to discuss a film documenting his life, and granted an interview to actor Sean Penn. Mexican authorities easily tracked, located and recaptured Guzmán. Now awaiting extradition to the United States, Guzmán's continued dominance of the Mexican drug trade seems unlikely.

7. THEY KNOW HOW TO ASSESS RISK AND WHEN TO TAKE OPPORTUNITIES: CHRISTOPHER COKE (JAMAICA)

Coke inherited leadership of the Shower Posse crime organisation from his father. Avoiding the limelight, he focused on expanding his drug enterprise's global reach and cultivating support and loyalty from the Tivoli Gardens community. Coke's dominance and success in the Jamaican drug trade can be attributed to his acquisition of firearms, political connections, and reputation as a community leader. Importing firearms from the United States enabled Coke not only to control and strengthen his organisation, but also to maintain his own power within it. Coke was a master at accurately assessing risks and taking opportunities when they arose. Coke promised votes to the Prime Minster of the Jamaican Labour Party in exchange for protection from criminal prosecution. He earned the support and loyalty of the Tivoli Gardens community by providing charitable donations, social programs, neighbourhood security, and jobs routed through his legitimate businesses. Ruling with a strategic combination of violence, corruption and philanthropy, at the height of his power Coke smuggled tons of marijuana and cocaine into Canada, the United States, the Caribbean and the United Kingdom.

Coke's downfall can be traced to a failure to lead. Despite his reputation as provider and protector, Coke failed to safeguard the Tivoli Gardens community from the violence that ensued when Jamaican law enforcement and military forces stormed Tivoli Gardens to arrest Coke. At least 76 people were killed in the Tivoli Gardens massacre. Coke surrendered to Jamaican authorities and was extradited to the United States. In 2012, he pleaded guilty to federal racketeering charges and was sentenced to a 23-year federal prison term.

CONCLUSION

The preface to this book questioned the merit of limiting our study to business models created by conventional visionary leaders such as Thomas Edison, Steve Jobs, Nikola Tesla and Bill Gates. This book proposes an alternative: that the most innovative and creative entrepreneurs operate on the fringe of business culture, outside the generally accepted confines of corporate organisation and governance. As pioneers of the underworld, drug Kingpins face unique challenges arising from the illegal nature of the drug trade. The inherently risky and unpredictable underworld inhabited by the Kingpins provides a wealth of diverse business lessons our mainstream leaders will never encounter and cannot teach.

True visionary leaders innovate and adapt business models that prosper without their guidance. They establish a workplace culture that encourages innovation in all aspects of the business. Forward-thinking leaders empower their employees to test the status quo and take calculated risks within a malleable environment. Forward-thinking leaders seize opportunities that break the rules of the traditional business model, provide new avenues for growth, and cultivate learning and independent thinking. A study of successful businesses, then, will necessarily include consideration of unconventional visionary leaders.

A review of the summaries of the Kingpins' respective careers demonstrates these visionary leaders shared common skills and used similar business practices that contributed to the success of their operations.

Lucas and Guzmán developed innovative methods to smuggle drugs into the United States.

Lucas, Escobar and Guzmán controlled specific aspects of distribution but outsourced the tasks they lacked expertise in handling.

Lucas and Ibrahim implemented diversity policies in the selection of their employees.

Sa, Escobar and Ibrahim developed relationships that provided business advantages.

Blanco and Coke inspired loyalty from their employees.

Escobar and Coke gained the respect of community members by making charitable donations and establishing social programs.

The Kingpins also shared common flaws and implemented similar business practices that contributed to their fall from power.

Blanco, Escobar and Guzmán used violence and intimidation to silence their rivals, a practice which ultimately resulted in the disruption or cessation of their business operations. Blanco was forced to abandon her Miami cocaine hub to flee retaliatory assassination attempts; Escobar's reign of terror against the politicians, journalists and civilians who exposed his connection to the drug trade outraged the public and provoked the Columbian Government to take action to contain him; identified as a participant in a cartel gunfight that caused the death of a prominent religious figure, Guzmán was subsequently arrested, convicted and imprisoned for his involvement in the violent attack.

Sa and Coke lost their power by exercising poor leadership in the face of adversity. Sa's soldiers began to doubt Sa's commitment to the Shan fight for freedom when Sa dedicated his efforts to protecting his interest in the opium trade. Similarly, Coke abandoned his role as leader of the Tivoli Gardens community when he failed to protect the community from the violent attack waged by

Jamaican authorities while executing a warrant for Coke's arrest.

Escobar and Guzmán ultimately fell from power because they sacrificed the interests of their drug enterprises to pursue personal aspirations.

Despite the immoral, destructive and violent culture of the illicit drug trade, drug Kingpins are – first and foremost – entrepreneurs and risk managers. The most successful Kingpins are true visionary leaders; they cannot survive or succeed without implementing effective business strategies and policies. By suspending our judgement of the drug dealer, we open our minds to the Kingpins' pioneering spirit – their skills, flaws, triumphs and downfalls are magnified by the volatile environment that shapes their enterprises.

ABOUT THE AUTHOR

Sarah Bartholomeusz is the founder and CEO of You Legal, a top-tier legal concierge service. You Legal is a new category of law firm providing corporate and commercial legal services to clients, including ASX-listed companies. You Legal's team members are based throughout Australia and in five other countries.

You Legal's *Growth Shield* provides clients with customised, watertight policy documentation. Policies are the strategic link between the vision for a business and its day-to-day operations. Growth Shield helps companies to future-proof their business by simply and transparently transforming their existing policy framework in a three-step process.

Sarah was awarded the prestigious Telstra Business Women's Award in the start-up category for South Australia in October 2015.

You Legal has appeared in the *Weekend Australian*, *CEO* Magazine, *The Advertiser*, InDaily, Law Management Hub, Short Press, Business News Australia, Legal Practice Intelligence, Australasian Lawyer and Dynamic Business.

Sarah's first book – *How to Avoid a Fall from Grace: Legal Lessons for Directors* – was ranked as a #1 bestseller on Amazon after its release in 2015, and she recently appeared on Channel 10 and 2UE discussing *Kingpin*.

Sarah is the Chair of the Catalyst Foundation Inc. and she serves on the South Australian Government's Education Standards Board.

Sarah loves to hear from readers. To connect:

Sarah Bartholomeusz
You Legal
sarah@youlegal.com.au
1300 870 661

You Legal

Facebook: https://www.facebook.com/Youlegal
Twitter: https://twitter.com/you_legal
LinkedIn: http://www.linkedin.com/company/you-legal
YouTube: https://www.youtube.com/channel/
　UCBCuX7FE1lZZh8oIRmPDayg

Sarah Bartholomeusz

Facebook: https://www.facebook.com/sarah.graves.397
Twitter: https://twitter.com/youlegal_sarah
LinkedIn: https://www.linkedin.com/in/
　sarah-graves-bartholomeusz-9179a948